School Subject-Integrated Reading Series

Reading for Subject

SECOND EDITION

2

Reading for Subject 2

Publisher Chung Kyudo
Authors Kim Seungmi, Yu Sunyeh, Han Jiyoung, Michael A. Putlack
Editors Seo Jeong-ah, Jeong Yeonsoon
Designers Koo Soojung, Forest

First published in December 2021
By Darakwon, Inc.
Darakwon Bldg., 211, Munbal-ro, Paju-si, Gyeonggi-do 10881
Republic of Korea
Tel: 82-2-736-2031 (Ext. 250)
Fax: 82-2-732-2037

ISBN 978-89-277-0897-1 54740
          978-89-277-0895-7 54740 (set)

www.darakwon.co.kr

Photo Credits
yiannisscheidt (p.18), Ziad (p.22), Seongbin Im (p.23), Piotrus (p.23), Nagel Photography (p.26), Ritu Manoj Jethani (p.38), neftali (p.39), Radu Bercan (p.39), Fedor Selivanov (p.50), Javen (p.51), spatuletail (p.79), Sanga Park (p.95) / www.shutterstock.com

Components Main Book / Workbook
10 9 8 7 6 5 4   24 25 26 27 28

School Subject-Integrated Reading Series

Reading for Subject

SECOND
EDITION

2

How to Use This Book

This book has 5 chapters, and each consists of 4 units. At the end of a chapter, there is a writing activity with a topic related to the last unit.

Student Book

Two warm-up questions to encourage students to think about the topic of the unit

QR code for listening to the reading passage

Finding the topic of each paragraph

BEFORE YOU READ

Students can learn the meaning of key vocabulary words by matching the words with their definitions.

Background knowledge about the topic is provided to help students better understand the main reading passage.

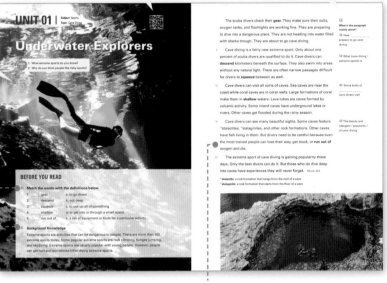

MAIN READING PASSAGE

Interesting, informative nonfiction reading passages covering various school subjects are provided.

CHECK YOUR COMPREHENSION

This section asks students to identify the main ideas and details and to make accurate inferences from the passage through 4 multiple-choice and 2 short-answer questions.

SHOW YOUR COMPREHENSION

Students can remember what they have read and organize the key information in the passage in a visual manner.

SUMMARIZE YOUR READING

Students can review and practice summarizing the key information in the passage.

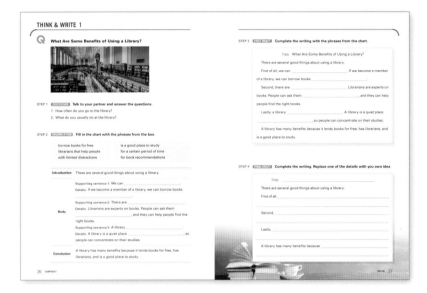

THINK & WRITE

Students can strengthen their writing skills by connecting ideas from the passage to their own lives. This also helps students prepare themselves for English performance assessments in school.

Workbook

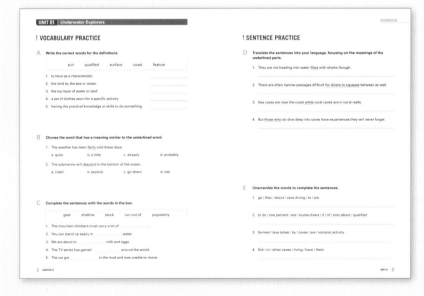

Students can review the vocabulary they learn in each unit. They can also review key structures in the passages by translating sentences and by putting words in the correct order.

Table of Contents

CHAPTER 01

UNIT	Title	Subject	Topic	Page
01	Underwater Explorers	Sports	Cave Diving	10
02	ID? My Ear	Life Science	Biometrics	14
03	$a^2+b^2=c^2$	Math	The Pythagorean Theorem	18
04	A Royal Library	Korean History	Kyujanggak	22
THINK & WRITE 1	What Are Some Benefits of Using a Library?			26

CHAPTER 02

UNIT	Title	Subject	Topic	Page
05	How To Get People on Your Side	Language	Persuasive Speech	30
06	How Glaciers Change the Land	Earth Science	Glacial Landforms	34
07	Art in Everyday Life	Art & Music	Andy Warhol	38
08	Get a Good Night's Sleep	Life Science	Sleep and Hormones	42
THINK & WRITE 2	What Can We Do for Our Health Every Day?			46

CHAPTER 03

UNIT	Title	Subject	Topic	Page
09	New Ways to See Art	Art & Music	Technology in Art	50
10	The Farms of the Future	Social Studies	Vertical Farming	54
11	For Only Good Dreams	History	Dream Catchers	58
12	The Ozone Layer Saves Itself?	Earth Science	The Ozone Layer	62
THINK & WRITE 3	How Can We Help Save the Earth?			66

CHAPTER 04

UNIT	Title	Subject	Topic	Page
13	The Secrets of Stars	Earth Science	Stars	70
14	The Other Stonehenges	History	Prehistoric Megaliths	74
15	Music in Famous Paintings	Art & Music	Music in Paintings	78
16	Helper or Bystander?	Social Studies	Good Samaritan Laws	82
THINK & WRITE 4	Why Do Many Students Not Volunteer?			86

CHAPTER 05

UNIT	Title	Subject	Topic	Page
17	Basic Geometry	Math	Lines	90
18	The Imjin War	Korean History	The Imjin War	94
19	Forests by the Shore	Life Science	Mangrove Forests	98
20	Is Early Childhood Education Effective?	Social Studies	Early Childhood Education	102
THINK & WRITE 5	How Can We Improve Our English?			106

CHAPTER
01

UNIT 01 Underwater Explorers_ Sports

UNIT 02 ID? My Ear_ Life Science

UNIT 03 $a^2 + b^2 = c^2$_ Math

UNIT 04 A Royal Library_ Korean History

THINK & WRITE 1

What Are Some Benefits of Using a Library?

UNIT 01 |

Subject Sports
Topic Cave Diving

Underwater Explorers

WARM UP

1. What extreme sports do you know?
2. Why do you think people like risky sports?

BEFORE YOU READ

A   Match the words with the definitions below.

1. _____ gear   a. to go down
2. _____ descend   b. not deep
3. _____ squeeze   c. to use up all of something
4. _____ shallow   d. to get into or through a small space
5. _____ run out of   e. a set of equipment or tools for a particular activity

B   Background Knowledge

Extreme sports are activities that can be dangerous to people. There are more than 100 extreme sports today. Some popular extreme sports are rock climbing, bungee jumping, and skydiving. Extreme sports are usually popular with young people. However, people can get hurt and sometimes killed doing extreme sports.

The scuba divers check their **gear**. They make sure their suits, oxygen tanks, and flashlights are working fine. They are preparing to dive into a dangerous place. They are not heading into water filled with sharks though. They are about to go cave diving.

5   Cave diving is a fairly new extreme sport. Only about one percent of scuba divers are qualified to do it. Cave divers can **descend** kilometers beneath the surface. They also swim into areas without any natural light. There are often narrow passages difficult for divers to **squeeze** between as well.

10   Cave divers can visit all sorts of caves. Sea caves are near the coast while coral caves are in coral reefs. Large formations of coral make them in **shallow** waters. Lava tubes are caves formed by volcanic activity. Some inland caves have underground lakes or rivers. Other caves get flooded during the rainy season.

15   Cave divers can see many beautiful sights. Some caves feature *stalactites, *stalagmites, and other rock formations. Other caves have fish living in them. But divers need to be careful because even the most trained people can lose their way, get stuck, or **run out of** oxygen and die.

20   The extreme sport of cave diving is gaining popularity these days. Only the best divers can do it. But those who do dive deep into caves have experiences they will never forget.   Words 228

* **stalactite** a rock formation that hangs from the roof of a cave
* **stalagmite** a rock formation that starts from the floor of a cave

Q
What is the paragraph mainly about?

P1 How _____ prepare to go cave diving

P2 What (cave diving / extreme sports) is

P3 Some kinds of _____ cave divers visit

P4 The beauty and (dangers / popularity) of cave diving

CHECK YOUR COMPREHENSION

Choose the best answers.

Main Idea **1** **What is the passage mainly about?**

    a. How to become a skilled cave diver

    b. What some popular caves for diving are

    c. Where cave divers go and what they see

    d. When cave diving began to become popular

Details **2** **According to the passage, which is NOT true about cave diving?**

    a. Divers often see sharks in caves.

    b. Divers can visit many types of caves.

    c. Some people die while they are doing it.

    d. Cave diving is becoming popular these day.

3 **Caves made by volcanic activity are called** _____.

    a. sea caves

    b. coral caves

    c. lava tubes

    d. inland caves

4 **What can be inferred from the passage?**

    a. Going cave diving can be expensive.

    b. People who like danger enjoy cave diving.

    c. People can take classes to learn to do cave diving.

    d. Cave diving is the most dangerous activity in the world.

Write the answers in complete sentences.

5 **How many scuba divers can do cave diving?**

_____

6 **Why do cave divers need to be careful?**

_____

SHOW YOUR COMPREHENSION

Fill in the chart with the phrases from the box.

Cave Diving

How to Do It	• Cave divers have suits, oxygen tanks, and flashlights. • Cave divers swim into areas ❶_____. • Cave divers squeeze ❷_____.
Where to Go and What to See	• Cave divers ❸_____, coral caves, lava tubes, and inland caves. • Some caves feature stalactites, stalagmites, and other rock formations. • Other caves ❹_____ in them.

have fish living	visit sea caves
between narrow passages	without natural light

SUMMARIZE YOUR READING

Complete the summary with the words from the box.

unforgettable	lava tubes	deep	formations
natural light	oxygen	qualified	gear

Scuba divers have to check their ❶_____ before diving into a dangerous place such as a cave. About one percent of scuba divers are ❷_____ to do cave diving. They swim ❸_____ beneath the surface into areas without any ❹_____. Scuba divers visit sea caves, coral caves, ❺_____, and inland caves. They see beautiful sights such as stalactites, stalagmites, and other rock ❻_____. But they can get lost and stuck or run out of ❼_____ and die. Cave diving is becoming popular these days, and cave divers have ❽_____ experiences.

ID? My Ear

WARM UP
1. What kind of ID do you have?
2. What can be used to identify a person?

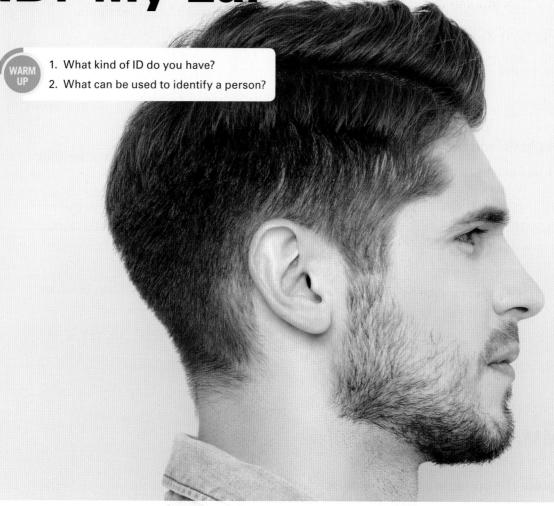

BEFORE YOU READ

A Match the words with the definitions below.

1. _____ identification   a. weakness

2. _____ measure   b. correct and true in every detail

3. _____ accurate   c. a person who says that something is not good

4. _____ limitation   d. to find the exact size or amount of something

5. _____ critic   e. proof of a person's name and other information

B Background Knowledge

Biometrics is a new kind of technology. It attempts to identify people based on human features. Some biometric scanners look at fingerprints, faces, and eyes. Others look at how people behave. For instance, some scanners can identify people by how they walk.

No more fingerprints as your ID! According to a report from a U.K. newspaper, the shape of your ear could be used as a means of **identification**.

A team of researchers from the University of Southampton in
5 the U.K. has studied the structure of the human ear. The researchers discovered that each person has his or her own unique ear shape. So they invented a system that scans ears. First, the system uses image rays to seek the curved parts of the ear. Next, it **measures** them. Then, it compares the scans with the shapes of the ears stored
10 in the system. Lastly, it finds out whose ears they are.

The results are 99.6 percent **accurate**. The research team presented the technique at the International Conference on Biometrics. Mark Nixon, the leader of the research team, says that the system can be used at airports to check people's IDs.

15 However, the system has some **limitations**. It does not work well when hair covers the ears, when there is not enough light, or when the angles are different. Some **critics** also say that there is no proof that the shapes of a person's ears stay the same.

Fingerprints are still used as IDs worldwide. But with more
20 research, the new technology using ear scans might work better for security systems. Words 219

Q

What is the paragraph mainly about?

P1 A new means of
_____

P2 (How / When) the ear scanner works

P3 (Where / When) the ear scanner can be used

P4 Some _____ of the system

P5 The possibility of using (fingerprints / ears) for identification

CHECK YOUR COMPREHENSION

Choose the best answers.

Main Idea **1** **What is the passage mainly about?**

    a. A new way to check IDs

    b. The structure of the human ear

    c. Body parts as unique as fingerprints

    d. The limitations of using fingerprints as IDs

Details **2** **According to the passage, which is true?**

    a. The ear-scanning system was made in the United States.

    b. The ear-scanning system is 100 percent accurate.

    c. The ear-scanning system is commonly used nowadays.

    d. In many countries, people use fingerprints to check IDs.

3 **During the scanning, the image rays seek the _____ of the ear.**

    a. size

    b. color

    c. rounded parts

    d. inner parts

4 **According to the passage, when does the ear-scanning system NOT work well?**

    a. When hair is behind a person's ear

    b. When there is little light

    c. When the angles are the same

    d. When the person it scans is very young

Write the answers in complete sentences.

5 **What did the researchers from a university in the U.K. discover about the human ear?**

_____

6 **What do some critics say about using ears as a means of identification?**

_____

SHOW YOUR COMPREHENSION

Fill in the chart with the phrases from the box.

Using Ears to Check IDs	
The Use of Ears for Identification	• Researchers discovered that ❶_____ are unique and invented a system that scans ears. • The results are ❷_____.
Limitations and Criticism	• The system does not work well when hair covers the ears, ❸_____, and the angles are different. • The shapes of a person's ears ❹_____.

may not stay the same	99.6 percent accurate
there is not enough light	the shapes of each person's ears

SUMMARIZE YOUR READING

Complete the summary with the words from the box.

fingerprints	scanning	change	limitations
identification	different	ears	airports

Ears could be used as a means of ❶_____. Usually, ❷_____ are used to check people's IDs. But a research team from a university in the U.K. found a way to use another part of the human body. It uses the curved parts of people's ❸_____. According to them, those parts are ❹_____ from person to person, so they can be used as IDs. The team invented a system for ❺_____ ears. The leader of the team says it can be used at ❻_____. But it is not used yet. The system has some ❼_____, and critics say that ear shapes may ❽_____.

$$a^2+b^2=c^2$$

1. What is the Pythagorean Theorem?
2. When do you use the Pythagorean Theorem?

Statue of Pythagoras ▶
in Greece

BEFORE YOU READ

A **Match the words with the definitions below.**

1. _____ equation　　a. a total
2. _____ right angle　　b. an angle of 90°
3. _____ sum　　c. the result of a calculation
4. _____ value　　d. a fact or rule that uses mathematical symbols
5. _____ formula　　e. a statement showing that two amounts are equal

B **Background Knowledge**

Pythagoras was a Greek mathematician who lived around 2,500 years ago. He came up with a proof about right triangles. It is called the Pythagorean Theorem. Pythagoras was also a philosopher. He believed that math could explain reality. Even today, people study his thoughts and beliefs.

$a^2 + b^2 = c^2$ This **equation** is the Pythagorean *Theorem or Pythagoras's Theorem. It was named after Pythagoras, a Greek mathematician.

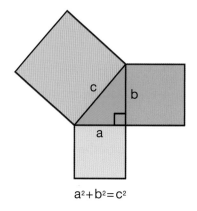

$a^2 + b^2 = c^2$

5   The theorem shows an interesting fact about right triangles. You can see a triangle on the right. The triangle has a **right angle**. Suppose you made three squares on each side (sides *a*, *b*, and *c*) of the triangle. Then, the
10 area of the square on the longest side (side *c*) is equal to the **sum** of the squares on the other two sides (sides *a* and *b*).

    Here is an example of this equation. Look at the triangle on the right. If side *a* is 3, side *b* is 4, and side *c* is 5, and
15 this triangle has a right angle, you can describe the triangle with the equation $3^2 + 4^2 = 5^2$. This becomes $9 + 16 = 25$. This theorem really works.

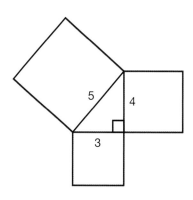

    The theorem is useful for calculating the length of the third side
20 of a triangle. Of course, you need to know the lengths of the other

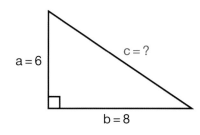

two sides. In addition, the triangle should have a right angle. Then, you can find the missing **value**. Try to find the length of side *c* in the triangle. Can you find the answer?

    Interestingly, Pythagoras is not the only person who discovered this theorem. Mathematicians from Babylon, Mesopotamia, India, and China also found this **formula**. Today, many people think the theorem is interesting, and it is often used in many fields.   Words 244

* **theorem** a rule or principle, especially in mathematics, that can be proved to be true

Q

What is the paragraph mainly about?

P2 What the

_____ is

P3 A(n) _____ of the Pythagorean Theorem

P4 Why the Pythagorean Theorem is (difficult / useful)

P5 (Where / When) the Pythagorean Theorem was discovered

CHECK YOUR COMPREHENSION

Choose the best answers.

Main Idea

1   What is the passage mainly about?

a. Interesting facts about shapes

b. The finders of the Pythagorean Theorem

c. Studies by mathematicians around the world

d. The relationship between the sides of a right triangle

Details

2   According to the passage, which is NOT true?

a. Pythagoras was originally the name of a formula.

b. The Pythagorean Theorem only applies to right triangles.

c. There are more than two finders of the Pythagorean Theorem.

d. The Pythagorean Theorem is still used in various fields.

3   A right triangle has _____.

a. two equal sides

b. three equal sides

c. a 90-degree angle

d. three equal angles

4   Which is NOT a place where someone discovered the Pythagorean Theorem?

a. China

b. France

c. Greece

d. Babylon

Write the answers in complete sentences.

5   What does the Pythagorean Theorem state about right triangles?

_____

6   In paragraph 4, what is the value of c?

_____

SHOW YOUR COMPREHENSION

Fill in the chart with the phrases from the box.

The Pythagorean Theorem	
Who Discovered It	• Pythagoras and ❶_____ from Babylon, Mesopotamia, India, and China discovered it.
What It Is	• In a right triangle, ❷_____ is equal to the sum of ❸_____.
When It Is Useful	• It is useful when you want to know ❹_____ of a right triangle.

the square on the longest side   the length of the third side

some mathematicians   the squares on the other two sides

SUMMARIZE YOUR READING

Complete the summary with the words from the box.

Pythagoras   right triangles   longest side   two sides

countries   sum   named after   length

The Pythagorean Theorem shows a fact about ❶_____. The formula is $a^2 + b^2 = c^2$. According to it, the square on the ❷_____ of a right triangle is the same as the ❸_____ of the squares on the two shorter sides. It was discovered by ❹_____, a Greek mathematician. So the theorem was ❺_____ him. But mathematicians from other ❻_____ also found it. By using it, we can determine the ❼_____ of the third side of a right triangle. Of course, this is only possible when we know the lengths of the other ❽_____.

A Royal Library

1. Why do you go to libraries?
2. How did people use libraries in the past?

BEFORE YOU READ

A **Match the words with the definitions below.**

1. _____ royal   a. valuable; important

2. _____ reform   b. relating to a king or queen

3. _____ scholar   c. happening once every year

4. _____ precious   d. a person with great knowledge

5. _____ annual   e. changes made to a law, social system, etc.

B **Background Knowledge**

Libraries are places with books and other materials, including newspapers, magazines, and videos. The oldest library was in the ancient city of Ebla, Syria, over 5,000 years ago. Since then, people have used libraries to read, to be educated, and to do research. Today, the world's largest library is the British Library in London. It contains over 170 million items from many countries.

The Kyujanggak was the **royal** library during the Joseon Dynasty. It was founded in Changdeok Palace by King Jeongjo in 1776. Its name comes from the imperial calligraphic works, the *kyujang*. It was a place where the writings of former kings and important books were kept.

The Kyujanggak was the center of the **reforms** of King Jeongjo. Although it started as a royal library, the king gradually changed it into a place for studying policies. He opened offices there for talented young **scholars** and did not consider anyone's political or social background. Among these young scholars was Jeong Yakyong, a great thinker in the Joseon Period.

The scholars were educated and tested for a certain period of time. After that, the king made them collect and study various writings and books from the past. He also took them on as political partners and made them responsible for political reforms. To protect the scholars from political pressure, the king only allowed official visits to the library.

The library was closed after the Gabo Reforms of 1894. Today, the official name of the library is the Kyujanggak Institute for Korean Studies. It is located at Seoul National University. It keeps **precious** Korean historical records, enables people to conduct research, and issues an **annual** journal *Kyujanggak*.   Words 213

Q

What is the paragraph mainly about?

P1 The founding of the

_____

P2 The Kyujanggak and the reforms of (King Jeongjo / Jeong Yakyong)

P3 What the

_____ at the Kyujanggak did

P4 What happened after the library was (closed / destroyed)

▲ King Jeongjo

▲ The collected works of King Jeongjo

CHECK YOUR COMPREHENSION

Choose the best answers.

Main Idea   1   **What is the passage mainly about?**

    a. The meaning of the *kyujang*

    b. The reforms made by King Jeongjo

    c. The roles of the Kyujanggak in history

    d. The scholars who studied at the Kyujanggak

Details   2   **According to the passage, which is true about the Kyujanggak?**

    a. It was named after King Jeongjo.

    b. It was once closed in the 1800s.

    c. It is still located in Changdeok Palace.

    d. It is still called the Kyujanggak.

3   **The Kyujanggak was a place for _____ as well as a library.**

    a. royal events

    b. the king to rest

    c. political reforms

    d. educating the people

4   **According to the passage, which is NOT true about King Jeongjo?**

    a. He founded the Kyujanggak.

    b. He wanted to reform the political situation.

    c. He had young scholars develop policies.

    d. He made the Gabo Reforms.

Write the answers in complete sentences.

5   **Why did the king only allow official visits to the library?**

_____

6   **What are the roles of the Kyujanggak today?**

_____

SHOW YOUR COMPREHENSION

Fill in the chart with the phrases from the box.

(Kyujanggak)

During the Joseon Dynasty	• was founded in Changdeok Palace by King Jeongjo in 1776 • was a place where ❶_____ and important books were kept • was the center of ❷_____
Present	• is located at ❸_____ • keeps historical records, enables people to conduct research, and ❹_____

issues a journal annually   the writings of former kings

Seoul National University   the reforms of King Jeongjo

SUMMARIZE YOUR READING

Complete the summary with the words from the box.

royal library   policies   former kings   King Jeongjo

roles   reforms   issues   political partners

The Kyujanggak was the ❶_____ during the Joseon Dynasty. It was built by ❷_____ in 1776. It was a place where the writings of ❸_____ and many important books were kept. The ❹_____ of the library have been changed over time. The founder, King Jeongjo, used the library to make ❺_____. He had young scholars there as ❻_____ and had them come up with new ❼_____. Later, the library was moved to Seoul National University. Today, important Korean historical records are kept there, and researchers conduct research there as well. The library also ❽_____ a journal entitled *Kyujanggak* every year.

THINK & WRITE 1

 What Are Some Benefits of Using a Library?

STEP 1 DISCUSSION **Talk to your partner and answer the questions.**

1. How often do you go to the library?

2. What do you usually do at the library?

STEP 2 ORGANIZATION **Fill in the chart with the phrases from the box.**

borrow books for free	is a good place to study
librarians that help people	for a certain period of time
with limited distractions	for book recommendations

Introduction	There are several good things about using a library.
Body	**Supporting sentence 1:** We can _____. **Details:** If we become a member of a library, we can borrow books _____. **Supporting sentence 2:** There are _____. **Details:** Librarians are experts on books. People can ask them _____, and they can help people find the right books. **Supporting sentence 3:** A library _____. **Details:** A library is a quiet place _____, so people can concentrate on their studies.
Conclusion	A library has many benefits because it lends books for free, has librarians, and is a good place to study.

FIRST DRAFT **Complete the writing with the phrases from the chart.**

Title   What Are Some Benefits of Using a Library?

There are several good things about using a library.

First of all, we can _____. If we become a member

of a library, we can borrow books _____.

Second, there are _____. Librarians are experts on

books. People can ask them _____, and they can help

people find the right books.

Lastly, a library _____. A library is a quiet place

_____, so people can concentrate on their studies.

A library has many benefits because it lends books for free, has librarians, and

is a good place to study.

FINAL DRAFT **Complete the writing. Replace one of the details with you own idea.**

Title   _____

There are several good things about using a library.

First of all, _____

_____

Second, _____

_____

Lastly, _____

_____

A library has many benefits because _____

_____

CHAPTER
02

UNIT 05 How To Get People on Your Side _ Language

UNIT 06 How Glaciers Change the Land _ Earth Science

UNIT 07 Art in Everyday Life _ Art & Music

UNIT 08 Get a Good Night's Sleep _ Life Science

THINK & WRITE 2

What Can We Do for Our Health Every Day?

How to Get People on Your Side

WARM UP

1. Have you ever persuaded people to do something?
2. Why do we need to persuade people?

BEFORE YOU READ

A **Match the words with the definitions below.**

1. _____ emotion
2. _____ sufficient
3. _____ statistics
4. _____ cite
5. _____ convince

a. enough; as much as one needs
b. a strong feeling
c. to mention as an example or proof
d. to make someone believe that something is true
e. facts or pieces of information shown in numbers

B **Background Knowledge**

People sometimes give speeches to persuade others to their opinions. People make persuasive speeches of fact, value, and policy. A persuasive speech could be about the need for school uniforms. Another could be about persuading people that video games are too violent. A third type of persuasive speech could be about the need to care for endangered animals.

Imagine that you must give a speech in front of a group of people to persuade them. It sounds difficult, doesn't it? Here are some tips you can use when you are making a persuasive speech.

First of all, the more you know about your audience, the better
5 your speech will be. Before you speak to your audience, you should learn their interests, expectations, and needs as much as possible. For instance, if you want to persuade people to do volunteer work in the community, focus on what types of work they can do. You could also talk about how they can make a difference.

10 Another thing is that you should try to make your audience feel a strong **emotion**. If you are talking about starving people in Africa, show them pictures of these people and their lives. In addition, try telling your audience a story that will inspire them. They will be more likely to remember your speech if you make them experience
15 a strong emotion.

Lastly, give your audience **sufficient** evidence. To make a good impression on them, you can use **statistics**, detailed examples, or newspaper articles. Imagine you are giving a speech about bullying. You can show some statistics or **cite** a newspaper article about how
20 many students are being bullied these days.

Try using these tips the next time you make a persuasive speech. They should help you **convince** your audience. Words 235

Q
What is the paragraph mainly about?

P2 What you should learn about your
_____

P3 Why (emotions / images) are important for your audience

P4 How to use
_____ to make a good impression

CHECK YOUR COMPREHENSION

Choose the best answers.

Main Idea

1 **What is the passage mainly about?**

a. Different types of speeches

b. How to make a persuasive speech

c. The importance of knowing your audience

d. How to persuade people to do volunteer work

Details

2 **Which is NOT mentioned as a tip for giving a persuasive speech?**

a. To learn as much as possible about your audience

b. To focus only on the positive aspects of your topic

c. To make your audience feel a strong emotion

d. To give your audience a lot of evidence

3 **How does the author explain the topic?**

a. By giving examples

b. By showing statistics

c. By citing a newspaper article

d. By comparing it with other types of speech

4 **According to the passage, which is true?**

a. You should use a lot of gestures for a persuasive speech.

b. You should always use pictures and stories in your speeches.

c. You should learn about what your audience wants and needs.

d. You will give a better speech if you know your audience in person.

Write the answers in complete sentences.

5 **How can we make a persuasive speech about starving people in Africa?**

_____

6 **What kinds of evidence can we use to make a good impression on our audience?**

_____

SHOW YOUR COMPREHENSION

Fill in the chart with the phrases from the box.

Making a Persuasive Speech

Learn about your audience.	e.g. Volunteering • Focus on what types of work people can do. • Talk about how they ❶_____.
Make your audience feel a strong emotion.	e.g. Starving people in Africa • ❷_____ these people and their lives. • Tell a story ❸_____.
Give your audience a lot of evidence.	e.g. Bullying • Show some statistics or ❹_____ about how many students are being bullied these days.

show pictures of   that will inspire them

can make a difference   cite a newspaper article

SUMMARIZE YOUR READING

Complete the summary with the words from the box.

persuasive speech   remember   statistics   need

audience   emotion   convince   evidence

Here are some useful tips when you want to make a(n) ❶_____. First, you should know your ❷_____. You should understand what they like or hate to do and what they want or ❸_____. Second, you should make your audience feel a strong ❹_____. The more you make your audience feel a strong emotion, the more they will ❺_____ your speech. Third, you should give lots of ❻_____ like ❼_____, detailed examples, or newspaper articles. If you want to ❽_____ a group of people, try using these three tips in your speech.

How Glaciers Change the Land

◀ Matterhorn

WARM UP
1. What is a glacier?
2. What are some landforms created by glaciers?

BEFORE YOU READ

A **Match the words with the definitions below.**

1. _____ contract   a. the top of a mountain

2. _____ retreat   b. to move backward; to gradually get smaller

3. _____ valley   c. to become smaller or lesser in size

4. _____ peak   d. water that is not salty, especially water from a lake or river

5. _____ fresh water   e. an area of low land between hills or mountains

B **Background Knowledge**

In some cold places, snow does not melt all year long. Over time, the snow builds up, becomes heavy, and turns to ice. This forms glaciers. Glaciers are mostly found in lands like Antarctica, Greenland, and Alaska. The largest glacier in the world is the Lambert-Fisher Glacier in Antarctica.

Glaciers are enormous sheets of ice and snow which form in cold areas. They are capable of moving in various directions as they expand and **contract**. During past ice ages, glaciers covered large parts of the Northern Hemisphere. When they advanced and

5 **retreated**, they changed the face of the Earth and created numerous landforms.

Fjords are one well-known type of glacial landform. They are found in places such as Chile, Greenland, and New Zealand, but the most famous fjords are in Norway. Fjords are deep, narrow

10 **valleys** flooded by seawater. The land around fjords has steep sides, and they connect with the ocean. Some fjords are thousands of meters deep in places.

Glaciers can also affect the shapes of mountains by forming horns. A horn is a sharp point at a mountain's **peak**. It usually forms

15 when three or more glaciers carve the sides of the mountain. The result is a sharp, narrow point. The Matterhorn in the Alps in Europe stands more than 4,400 meters high. The actions of several glaciers created its horn.

Lakes can be formed by glaciers as well. The Great Lakes in the

20 United States and Canada are five huge lakes containing around 20 percent of the world's liquid **fresh water**. Retreating glaciers formed these glacial lakes—and many others—thousands of years ago. Words 219

Q

What is the paragraph mainly about?

P1 What _____ are and how they created landforms

P2 What fjords are and (when / where) they are found

P3 How glaciers can affect the (shapes / heights) of mountains

P4 _____ formed by glaciers

▲ Fjords in Norway

CHECK YOUR COMPREHENSION

Choose the best answers.

<u>Main Idea</u>   **1**   **What is the passage mainly about?**

   a. Landforms created by glaciers

   b. Glaciers and the way they form

   c. Fjords and horns around the world

   d. Bodies of water formed by glaciers

<u>Details</u>   **2**   **According to the passage, which is NOT true about fjords?**

   a. They are formed deep in the oceans.

   b. They can be thousands of meters deep.

   c. They are found in many places around the world.

   d. They are valleys flooded by the sea.

3   **Glaciers can create lakes when they** _____.

   a. form

   b. retreat

   c. advance

   d. become larger

4   **What can be inferred from the passage?**

   a. There are few glaciers around the world today.

   b. Glaciers affected Norway the most in the world.

   c. Some glaciers are still creating lakes these days.

   d. The Earth would look different without glaciers.

Write the answers in complete sentences.

5   **What is a horn?**

   _____

6   **How much water do the Great Lakes contain?**

   _____

SHOW YOUR COMPREHENSION

Fill in the chart with the phrases from the box.

Glacial Landforms

Glaciers	• They are ❶_____ which form in cold areas. • They ❷_____ when they advanced and retreated.
Glacial Landforms	• Fjords are ❸_____ flooded by seawater and connect with the ocean. • Horns are ❹_____ that form when glaciers carve the sides of mountains. • Retreating glaciers can form glacial lakes.

deep, narrow valleys   sharp points on mountain peaks

changed the face of the Earth   enormous sheets of ice and snow

SUMMARIZE YOUR READING

Complete the summary with the words from the box.

liquid fresh water   fjords   retreated   peak

horn   enormous   sides   seawater

Glaciers are ❶_____ sheets of ice and snow that once covered much of the Northern Hemisphere. When they advanced and ❷_____ during past ice ages, they created numerous landforms. There are many ❸_____ in Norway and other places. They are deep, narrow valleys with steep sides and are filled with ❹_____. A horn is a sharp point at a mountain's ❺_____. It forms when glaciers carve the ❻_____ of a mountain. The Matterhorn is one famous ❼_____. The Great Lakes in the United States and Canada were formed by glaciers. The lakes contain around 20 percent of the world's ❽_____.

Art in Everyday Life

WARM UP

1. Have you ever seen Andy Warhol's art?
2. What characteristics can you find in his art?

BEFORE YOU READ

A **Match the words with the definitions below.**

1. _____ object   a. a famous person
2. _____ celebrity   b. ordinary people in society
3. _____ public   c. a display of art or other similar things
4. _____ consumerism   d. a thing that you can see and touch but is not alive
5. _____ exhibition   e. the belief that it is good to buy and use a lot of goods

B **Background Knowledge**

The Pop Art Movement began in the United States and England in the 1950s. Artists such as Andy Warhol and Roy Lichtenstein were famous pop artists. They used commercial items and cultural icons to make art. Artists in the movement were influenced by the popular—or pop—culture of their time.

What do you see in the picture? There is a stamp. The image of Marilyn Monroe, a famous actress, is from the artwork *Marilyn Monroe* by Andy Warhol.

5   This is pop art. It uses **objects** in everyday life and images from mass media and popular culture. Andy Warhol was the most famous pop artist in the 1960s. He made silkscreen artwork which featured dollar bills, detergent
10 boxes, soup cans, bananas, and other similar objects. He also put **celebrities** like Marilyn Monroe, Elvis Presley, and Muhammad Ali on his canvases. He said it was great that the richest and the poorest bought the same things in America. For example, a famous actor pays the same amount of money as a poor man does to buy
15 a Coke. By using popular culture, he wanted to get closer to the **public**. That was why he made pop art.

    During the 1960s, Warhol founded a studio called the Factory. It became a gathering place for artists, writers, musicians, and celebrities. Warhol and his works became more famous. However,
20 he also had critics. They attacked Warhol by saying that his art represented **consumerism**. At that time, American art was changing greatly, and he was at the center of it.

    Since Warhol died, many books, films, and **exhibitions** have looked back at him and his art. Nowadays, his work is popular with collectors and is very valuable.   Words 231

Q

What is the paragraph mainly about?

P1 A work of art featuring (Andy Warhol / Marilyn Monroe)

P2 The _____ that Andy Warhol created

P3 What happened to Warhol after he became _____

P4 How people consider Warhol and his (books / works)

CHECK YOUR COMPREHENSION

Choose the best answers.

Main Idea

1 **What is the passage mainly about?**

   a. The history of pop art

   b. American art in the 1960s

   c. The most famous American artists

   d. Pop art and the most famous pop artist

Details

2 **According to the passage, which is true about Andy Warhol?**

   a. He designed many everyday objects.

   b. He was not famous during his lifetime.

   c. He liked to use celebrities in his artwork.

   d. He sold his artwork only to wealthy people.

3 **The Factory was a place where** _____.

   a. Warhol's artwork was sold

   b. artists and celebrities met

   c. critics gathered

   d. films about Warhol were showed

4 **Which are NOT mentioned as things people have used to remember Andy Warhol?**

   a. Books

   b. Films

   c. Stamps

   d. Exhibitions

Write the answers in complete sentences.

5 **Why did Andy Warhol make pop art?**

   _____

6 **How did critics attack Warhol?**

   _____

SHOW YOUR COMPREHENSION

Fill in the chart with the phrases from the box.

Andy Warhol

What He Did	• He used ❶_____ in his art. • He founded the studio called the Factory. • He was at the center of ❷_____.
Criticism	• His art ❸_____.
Influence	• There have been books, films, and exhibitions about him. • His works are still ❹_____.

American art in the 1960s   everyday objects and celebrities

very popular and valuable   represented consumerism

SUMMARIZE YOUR READING

Complete the summary with the words from the box.

pop artists   consumerism   popular culture   changed

the Factory   celebrities   died   valuable

Andy Warhol is one of the most famous ❶_____. He used common things

and ❷_____ in his art. He thought that by using ❸_____, he could

reach the public. During the 1960s, Warhol founded a studio, ❹_____, and

artists, writers, musicians, and celebrities gathered there. There were some critics who

said that his works represented ❺_____. But he became very famous and

❻_____ the American art world. Since he ❼_____, he has been

remembered through books, films, and exhibitions. His artwork is still very popular and

❽_____.

UNIT 08 |

Subject Life Science
Topic Sleep and Hormones

Get a Good Night's Sleep

1. How much do you sleep every night?
2. What happens if you don't get enough sleep?

BEFORE YOU READ

A **Match the words with the definitions below.**

1. _____ appetite   a. not useful

2. _____ suppress   b. a desire for food

3. _____ lack   c. to stop or slow down

4. _____ result in   d. to cause something to happen

5. _____ useless   e. not to have or not to have enough of something

B **Background Knowledge**

Sleep is very important. Everyone, especially teenagers, needs to sleep. Most doctors recommend that teenagers sleep eight to ten hours a night. Teenagers who get enough sleep have better physical and mental health. They learn more at school and pay attention in class better. They have good memories, too.

Medical researchers say that if people do not sleep enough, they will gain weight. Is there a relationship between sleep and weight?

Sleep and **appetite** hormones are closely linked. Those hormones are leptin and ghrelin. They control how hungry or full
5 people feel. Leptin **suppresses** appetite by making people feel full. Ghrelin, on the other hand, increases appetite by making people feel hungry.

When people do not get enough sleep, they have less leptin. Then they will not feel full even after they eat enough. People also
10 have more ghrelin if they **lack** sleep. When this happens, they will want to eat more. So they can easily gain weight. Because of these facts, you may think that getting a lot of sleep will **result in** weight loss. However, this is only true for people who do not sleep enough.

The human body needs at least 7 hours of sleep a day. According
15 to Dr. Michael Breus, people who already get enough sleep will not lose weight. But 2 more hours of sleep will result in weight loss for people who usually sleep for fewer than 5 hours. In addition, the quality of sleep is important. For example, getting 7 hours of bad sleep a night is **useless**. If people have difficulty sleeping deeply, getting enough sleep will not help them lose weight.   Words 222

Q
What is the paragraph mainly about?

P2 Two _____ hormones and their effects on the body

P3 How sleeping less can make people (gain / lose) weight

P4 How the quantity and _____ of sleep affect weight loss

CHECK YOUR COMPREHENSION

Choose the best answers.

<u>Main Idea</u>   1   **What is the passage mainly about?**

    a. How to lose weight

    b. How to sleep better at night

    c. Important hormones in the body

    d. The relationship between sleep and weight

<u>Details</u>   2   **According to the passage, which is NOT true?**

    a. Sleep affects two appetite hormones.

    b. Leptin is a hormone that makes people feel full.

    c. Ghrelin is a hormone that makes people feel hungry.

    d. People should sleep as much as possible to lose weight.

3   **If your body has less leptin, _____.**

    a. you will lose weight

    b. you will feel sleepy all day

    c. you will not sleep well at night

    d. you will not feel full after a meal

4   **Getting little sleep is related to _____.**

    a. lower levels of leptin and lower levels of ghrelin

    b. higher levels of leptin and lower levels of ghrelin

    c. lower levels of leptin and higher levels of ghrelin

    d. higher levels of leptin and higher levels of ghrelin

Write the answers in complete sentences.

5   **According to the passage, how many hours of sleep does the human body need?**

_____

6   **Beside getting enough sleep, what is important to help people lose weight?**

_____

SHOW YOUR COMPREHENSION

Fill in the chart with the phrases from the box.

Sleep and Weight

Two Appetite Hormones	• ❶_____ by making people feel full. • Ghrelin increases appetite by making people feel hungry.
Sleep and Weight	• When people lack sleep, they have less leptin and more ghrelin. • Then they ❷_____ and want to eat more. • As a result, ❸_____.
The Quantity and Quality of Sleep	• The human body needs at least 7 hours of sleep a day. • ❹_____, they will not lose weight.

they can easily gain weight   will not feel full after a meal

leptin suppresses appetite   if people do not sleep deeply

SUMMARIZE YOUR READING

Complete the summary with the words from the box.

suppresses   bad sleep   lose weight   link

gain weight   increases   quality   full

Researchers say that people can ❶_____ if they do not sleep enough. There is a close ❷_____ between sleep and the appetite hormones leptin and ghrelin. Leptin ❸_____ appetite while ghrelin ❹_____ it. If people lack sleep, their body has less leptin and more ghrelin. Then, they will not feel ❺_____ after a meal and will want to eat more. This will make them gain weight. However, if people get enough sleep, it will help them ❻_____. In addition, the ❼_____ of sleep is important. Getting ❽_____ does not help people lose weight even if they sleep enough.

THINK & WRITE 2

What Can We Do for Our Health Every Day?

STEP 1 **DISCUSSION** **Talk to your partner and answer the questions.**

1. How can we improve our health?

2. How can those activities help us?

STEP 2 **ORGANIZATION** **Fill in the chart with the phrases from the box.**

exercise more often	for their bodies to work well
take vitamin supplements	make people much healthier
are much better than fast food	food that is nutritious and healthy

Introduction	We can do many things to improve our health every day.
Body	**Supporting sentence 1:** We can eat _____. **Details:** Fruits and vegetables _____. They can help people lose weight. **Supporting sentence 2:** We can also _____. **Details:** Jogging, running, and aerobics are great ways to exercise. They can _____. **Supporting sentence 3:** We can _____ at times. **Details:** Vitamin supplements can help people get the necessary vitamins _____.
Conclusion	We can improve our health by eating nutritious food, doing exercise, and taking vitamins at times.

FIRST DRAFT **Complete the writing with the phrases from the chart.**

Title　What Can We Do for Our Health Every Day?

We can do many things to improve our health every day.

　First, we can eat _____. Fruits and vegetables

_____. They can help people lose weight.

　Second, we can also _____. Jogging, running, and

aerobics are great ways to exercise. They can _____.

　Lastly, we can _____ at times. Vitamin supplements

can help people get the necessary vitamins _____.

　We can improve our health by eating nutritious food, doing exercise, and

taking vitamins at times.

STEP 4　**FINAL DRAFT** **Complete the writing. Replace one of the details with you own idea.**

Title　_____

We can do many things to improve our health every day.

First, _____

_____

Second, _____

_____

Lastly, _____

_____

We can improve our health by _____

_____

CHAPTER
03

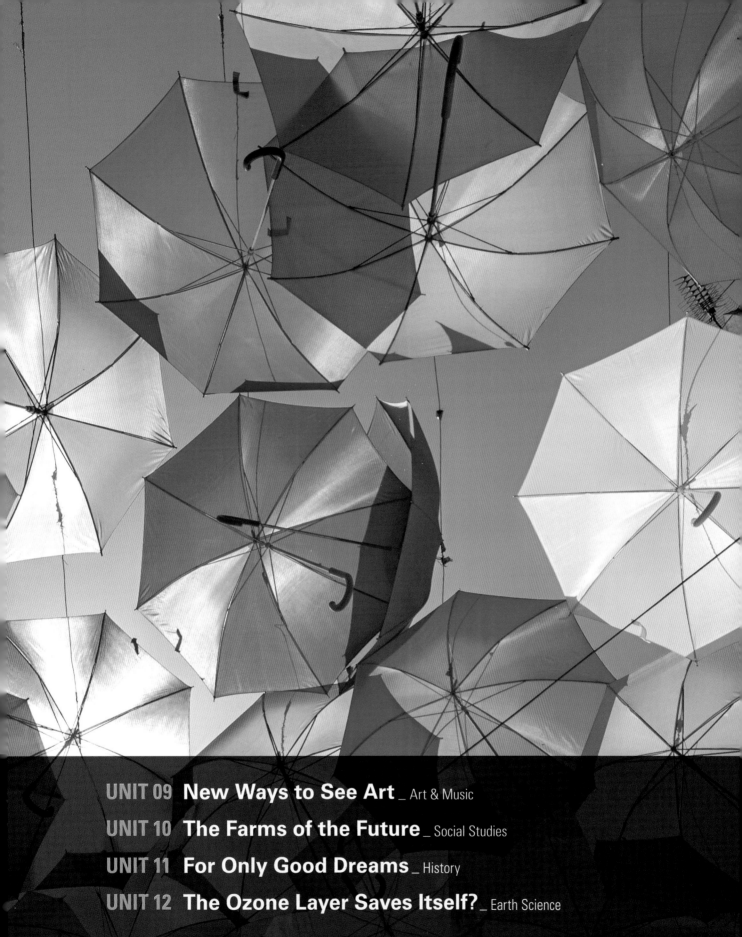

UNIT 09 **New Ways to See Art** _ Art & Music

UNIT 10 **The Farms of the Future** _ Social Studies

UNIT 11 **For Only Good Dreams** _ History

UNIT 12 **The Ozone Layer Saves Itself?** _ Earth Science

THINK & WRITE 3
How Can We Help Save the Earth?

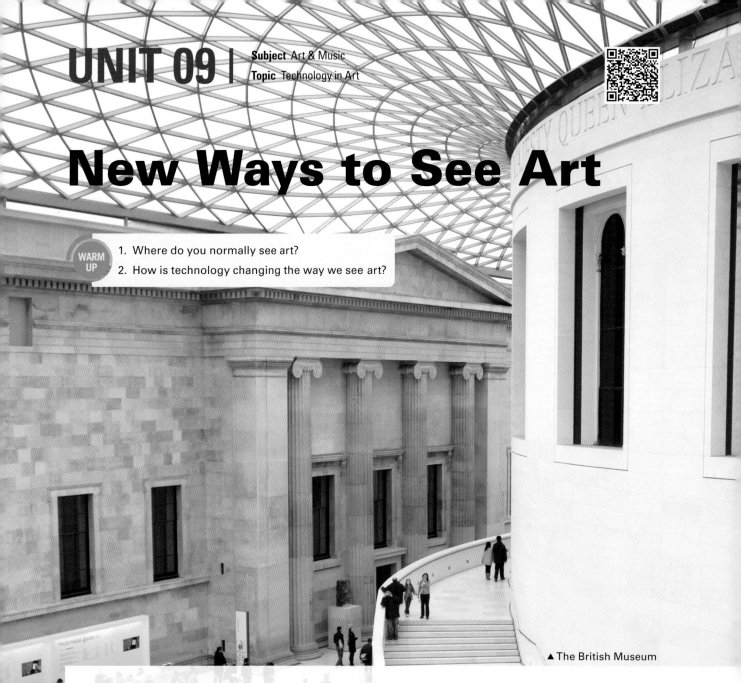

UNIT 09 | **Subject** Art & Music
Topic Technology in Art

New Ways to See Art

WARM UP

1. Where do you normally see art?
2. How is technology changing the way we see art?

▲ The British Museum

BEFORE YOU READ

A **Match the words with the definitions below.**

1. _____ in person   a. near

2. _____ up close   b. personally; physically present

3. _____ explore   c. a preserved, wrapped-up body

4. _____ statue   d. to travel around a place to find out what it is like

5. _____ mummy   e. a figure of a person or animal made of stone, metal, etc.

B **Background Knowledge**

Technology is being used in the art world nowadays. Software lets people draw pictures and make designs on computers. Images of art are available online, so people can view art with computers. Some people even use artificial intelligence (AI) to create art. AI can make art without help from humans.

Leonardo, Michelangelo, Cezanne, and Renoir made some of history's greatest art. Their works—and those of others—are in museums and art galleries. But most people cannot go to those places **in person**. They may lack the money, time, or ability to travel.
5　There are other ways to see these works **up close** though.

Museums and galleries have been putting their collections online recently. They then make their art available in virtual reality (VR) and augmented reality (AR). VR creates a computer-generated world and lets people **explore** it. AR takes digital images and puts
10　them into the real world around people.

Both methods allow people to view art. People interested in Renaissance art can take a virtual tour of the Vatican Museums. They have 360-degree access to paintings, **statues**, and other works of art. They can get a guided, narrated tour as well.

15　People can use VR to see the Rosetta Stone and **mummies** from Egypt at the British Museum. Other works of art there are also available. Those who prefer modern art can tour the Guggenheim in Bilbao, Spain. All they need is a desktop computer, laptop, or smartphone.

20　Thanks to modern technology, it is not necessary to travel to see art anymore. Instead, people can use VR and AR. Then, they can go on tours that are almost like the real thing.　Words 224

Q

What is the paragraph mainly about?

P1 (When / Why) most people cannot visit museums and art galleries

P2 What virtual reality and _____ are

P3 What people can see on a(n) (in-person / virtual) tour of the Vatican Museums

P4 Some other _____ that provide VR tours

P5 How modern technology helps people see _____

▲ The Vatican Museum

CHECK YOUR COMPREHENSION

Choose the best answers.

Main Idea 1 **What is the passage mainly about?**

    a. The uses of VR and AR in art

    b. The world's best art museums

    c. Modern technology and artists

    d. The most famous art in the world

Details 2 **What does augmented reality do?**

    a. It creates a new world for people to see.

    b. It lets people explore a different type of reality.

    c. It puts digital images into the real world.

    d. It takes the real world and makes it look better.

3 **People can tour the Guggenheim by using _____.**

    a. a television

    b. a smartphone

    c. a digital camera

    d. a free audio guide

4 **What can be inferred from the passage?**

    a. Art lovers prefer using VR to seeing art in person.

    b. Some museums have closed due to a lack of visitors.

    c. More people can see art thanks to modern technology.

    d. It costs money for people to take VR tours of museums.

Write the answers in complete sentences.

5 **What does virtual reality do?**

_____

6 **What can people see at the British Museum by using VR?**

_____

SHOW YOUR COMPREHENSION

Fill in the chart with the phrases from the box.

> **VR and AR in Art**

What They Are	• VR creates ❶_____ and lets people explore it. • AR takes digital images and ❷_____ around people.
How People Can Use Them to See Art	• People ❸_____ of the Vatican Museums. • People can use VR to see the Rosetta Stone and mummies from Egypt at the British Museum. • People can see modern art at the Guggenheim in Bilbao, Spain, ❹_____, laptop, or smartphone.

with a desktop computer   a computer-generated world

can take a virtual tour   puts them into the real world

SUMMARIZE YOUR READING

Complete the summary with the words from the box.

in person	travel	Renaissance art	Egypt
modern art	collections	tours	VR

Many people cannot see the world's greatest art because they cannot visit museums ❶_____. But nowadays, museums and art galleries are putting their ❷_____ online. So people can use ❸_____ and AR to see art. People can view ❹_____ such as paintings and statues at the Vatican Museums. They can see artwork from ❺_____ at the British Museum. And they can see ❻_____ at the Guggenheim. Because of modern technology, people do not have to ❼_____ to see art anymore. They can just go on VR and AR ❽_____.

UNIT 10 |

Subject Social Studies
Topic Vertical Farming

The Farms of the Future

WARM UP
1. Where do farmers grow crops?
2. How will farming change in the future?

BEFORE YOU READ

A Match the words with the definitions below.

1. _____ billion   a. ordinary; not special
2. _____ urbanization   b. plants grown on a farm
3. _____ crop   c. 1,000,000,000; one thousand million
4. _____ exposure   d. the process of becoming like a city
5. _____ commonplace   e. the condition of being open to something

B Background Knowledge

As cities get bigger, people are turning to urban farming. Urban farming is growing or producing food in a city environment. In small gardens and on rooftops, people grow fruits, vegetables, grains, and herbs. Vertical farms, which are indoors, are becoming popular, too. Nowadays, people have many ways to grow their own food in cities.

The world's population is currently more than seven **billion** people. This number is rising steadily every year. Experts expect it will increase to nine billion people by the year 2050. All of these people need to eat. But there is a big problem. Due to industrial development

5 and **urbanization**, the amount of farmland is decreasing. So people need to produce more food on smaller amounts of land.

To solve this problem, *vertical farming was invented. A vertical farm is like a greenhouse. Yet there is an important difference. Greenhouses have just one level while vertical farms have many

10 levels. For instance, in Suwon, South Korea, there is a 3-story vertical farm. In nearby Yongin, there is a 7-story vertical farm. There are vertical farms in many other countries, too.

Vertical farming has a number of advantages. Vertical farms operate indoors, so the weather does not affect the **crops** at all. This

15 allows crops to grow all year round. Vertical farms also use less water because it is recycled within the building. In addition, because of their well-controlled environments, there is less **exposure** to harmful insects and diseases. Finally, people can produce more food in limited amounts of space, which is the primary goal of

20 vertical farming.

Thanks to vertical farms, people in cities are now able to grow their own crops. Vertical farms are just getting started. But they will be **commonplace** in the future.   Words 235

* **vertical farming** the practice of growing crops on vertically stacked layers

---

Q

What is the paragraph mainly about?

P1 What problem population growth and the loss of

_____ are

causing

P2 What (a greenhouse / vertical farming) is

P3 Some

_____ of

vertical farming

P4 How vertical farms are helping people in (cities / the countryside)

CHECK YOUR COMPREHENSION

Choose the best answers.

Main Idea   1   **What is the passage mainly about?**

a. A new way to grow more food

b. Foods people will eat in the future

c. Some effects of rapid population growth

d. Advantages and disadvantages of vertical farming

Details   2   **According to the passage, what is expected in the future?**

a. The world's population will decrease.

b. More people will live in the countryside.

c. There will not be enough food for everyone.

d. There will be less farmland available to grow food.

3   **Which is NOT mentioned as an advantage of vertical farming?**

a. People can grow crops all year round.

b. It is cheaper than other farming methods.

c. Crops are less exposed to harmful insects and diseases.

d. People can produce more food in limited amounts of space.

4   **What can be inferred about vertical farms?**

a. They usually rely on natural sunlight.

b. Korea has the largest vertical farms in the world.

c. They grow the same amount of food as in greenhouses.

d. They are likely to be located in or near cities.

Write the answers in complete sentences.

5   **What is the difference between greenhouses and vertical farms?**

_____

6   **Why does the weather not affect crops in vertical farms?**

_____

SHOW YOUR COMPREHENSION

Fill in the chart with the phrases from the box.

Vertical Farming

Background	• The world's population is increasing every year. • ❶_____ is decreasing. • People need to produce more food on smaller amounts of land.
Greenhouses vs. Vertical Farms	• Greenhouses have one level while vertical farms ❷_____.
Advantages	• People can ❸_____. • Vertical farms use less water because it is recycled. • Crops are less exposed to ❹_____. • People can produce more food in limited amounts of space.

have many levels   the amount of farmland

grow crops all year round   harmful insects and diseases

SUMMARIZE YOUR READING

Complete the summary with the words from the box.

population   popular   less water   fewer

smaller   farmland   levels   indoors

The world's ❶_____ is growing steadily, but the amount of ❷_____ is decreasing. Vertical farming was invented to help people grow more food on ❸_____ amounts of land. Vertical farms are similar to greenhouses, but they have many ❹_____. Vertical farms have lots of advantages. As the farms are ❺_____, people can grow crops all year round. They also use ❻_____ by using recycled water. Due to their well-controlled environments, there are ❼_____ harmful insects and diseases. Vertical farms will become more and more ❽_____ worldwide.

UNIT 11 |
Subject History
Topic Dream Catchers

For Only Good Dreams

WARM UP
1. How often do you dream?
2. What do you usually dream about?

BEFORE YOU READ

A Match the words with the definitions below.

1. _____ tribe   a. to disappear suddenly
2. _____ keep away   b. a small, thin branch of a tree
3. _____ hoop   c. a social group in a traditional society
4. _____ twig   d. to prevent something from coming
5. _____ vanish   e. a circular band of wood, metal, etc.

B Background Knowledge

Native Americans are the people who lived in the Americas before the Europeans began arriving in the late 1400s. There were hundreds of tribes living in North and South America. They had their own languages and cultures. Many were nomadic, but others farmed the land and lived in the same place.

Many years before the Europeans discovered North America, people were already living all over the continent. There were a large number of different **tribes** of people. These tribes had their own languages, customs, and cultures. One of the largest groups
5 of Native Americans was the Ojibwe tribe. The people in this tribe lived in parts of both modern-day Canada and the United States. One important part of their culture was the dream catcher.

The Ojibwe people knew that everyone dreamed. They also knew that dreams could be good or bad. They welcomed good
10 dreams but wanted to prevent people from having bad dreams. For that reason, they invented the dream catcher. The dream catcher was a kind of *talisman. The Ojibwe people believed it could **keep away** bad dreams.

There were many types of dream catchers. They were all based
15 on a **hoop** design. The hoop was typically a **twig** from a *willow tree that was bent into a circle. String was woven in the center, so it looked like a spider web. Then, the hoop was decorated with a variety of items, such as feathers, beads, arrowheads, and other items that were important to them.

20 Once the dream catcher was completed, it was placed over a person's bed. It would let good dreams pass through the holes in the web while the person slept. But it caught bad dreams and held them until morning. Then, the bad dreams **vanished** when the sun came up. Words 245

*talisman an object that is believed to have magic powers to protect a person or bring good luck
*willow (tree) a tree with long, thin branches and narrow leaves that grows near water

Q
What is the paragraph mainly about?
P1 Who lived in North America before

_____

discovered it

P2 Why the Ojibwe people invented the

_____

P3 How the dream catcher was (made / used)

P4 How the dream catcher (worked / became popular)

CHECK YOUR COMPREHENSION

Choose the best answers.

Main Idea **1** **What is the passage mainly about?**

   a. Native American cultures

   b. Items that brings good luck

   c. How to make a dream catcher

   d. A talisman the Ojibwe people used

Details **2** **According to the passage, which is true?**

   a. The Ojibwe people lived in Europe.

   b. The Ojibwe people spoke English.

   c. The Ojibwe people had their own customs.

   d. The Ojibwe tribe was very small.

3 **The Ojibwe people used dream catchers _____.**

   a. to entertain babies

   b. to decorate their homes

   c. to give to others as presents

   d. to keep safe from bad dreams

4 **Which is NOT mentioned about the dream catcher?**

   a. Who invented it

   b. How it was made

   c. Why it is popular today

   d. What materials are needed to make it

Write the answers in complete sentences.

5 **Where was the dream catcher placed?**

_____

6 **What happened to bad dreams caught in the dream catcher?**

_____

SHOW YOUR COMPREHENSION

Fill in the chart with the phrases from the box.

The Dream Catcher

Where It Came From	• was invented by the Ojibwe people • used as a talisman to ❶_____
How It Was Made	• was made from ❷_____ that was bent into a circle • ❸_____ so it looked like a spider web • was decorated with feathers, beads, and arrowheads
How It Worked	• was placed over a person's bed • would let good dreams pass through but catch bad dreams ❹_____ .

until the sun came up   a twig from a willow tree

had string woven in the center   keep away bad dreams

SUMMARIZE YOUR READING

Complete the summary with the words from the box.

keep away	pass through	feathers	hoop
vanished	bed	string	Native Americans

The Ojibwe tribe was one of the largest groups of ❶_____ in North America. The Ojibwe people made dream catchers to ❷_____ bad dreams. Dream catchers were all based on a ❸_____ design. The hoop was made of a willow tree branch and had ❹_____ woven in the center. It was decorated with items like ❺_____, beads, and arrowheads. The dream catcher was hung over a person's ❻_____. The Ojibwe people believed that it let good dreams ❼_____ while it caught bad dreams. When the sun came up, the bad dreams ❽_____.

The Ozone Layer Saves Itself?

WARM UP

1. Where is the ozone layer?
2. Why is the ozone layer important?

BEFORE YOU READ

A **Match the words with the definitions below.**

1. _____ atmosphere   a. to fix
2. _____ layer   b. the air that surrounds the Earth
3. _____ atom   c. the smallest unit of any substance
4. _____ concentration   d. a sheet of something that lies over another thing
5 _____ repair   e. the amount of substance in a liquid or in another substance

B **Background Knowledge**

The Earth's atmosphere is made up of different layers. The one closest to the ground is the troposphere. It contains the oxygen people need to survive. The stratosphere is the next layer. The ozone layer is in it. The mesosphere, the thermosphere, and the exosphere are the other three layers.

The Earth's **atmosphere** consists of the air that covers the planet from the surface to outer space. The atmosphere can be divided into several different **layers**. The ozone layer is in the stratosphere, the second layer of the Earth's atmosphere.

5　　The oxygen that we breathe is made up of two **atoms** (O_2). Ozone, however, forms when three atoms of oxygen join together (O_3). The ozone layer is a thin layer in the atmosphere with a high **concentration** of ozone gas. It is mostly found between 20 and 30 kilometers above the Earth's surface.

10　　The ozone layer is important for one main reason. This layer protects the Earth from the harmful ultraviolet rays of the sun. It is these ultraviolet rays that cause people to get sunburns and skin cancer. Without the ozone layer, ultraviolet rays would hurt or kill most of the plants and animals that live on the planet.

15　　In recent years, scientists have discovered that some parts of the ozone layer have holes. For instance, there are some holes in the ozone layer above the Arctic. Fortunately, it appears that the ozone layer can **repair** itself. The holes sometimes increase in size, yet they also decrease in size. So long as the ozone layer exists, humans—and other forms of life—will be safe.　Words 216

Q
What is the paragraph mainly about?

P1 What the Earth's _____ consists of

P2 What (an atom / the ozone layer) is

P3 Why the ozone layer is (important / harmful)

P4 What scientists have _____ about the ozone layer

CHECK YOUR COMPREHENSION

Choose the best answers.

Main Idea **1** **What is the passage mainly about?**

a. Some facts about the ozone layer

b. The layers of the Earth's atmosphere

c. The harmful effects of the sun's ultraviolet rays

d. How to prevent the destruction of the ozone layer

Details **2** **The ozone layer is mainly found _____.**

a. in outer space

b. above the Arctic

c. on the Earth's surface

d. in the Earth's atmosphere

3 **According to the passage, which is NOT true?**

a. Ozone consists of oxygen.

b. The ozone layer can heal itself.

c. The ozone layer is harmful to plants.

d. The ozone layer is necessary for humans.

4 **Which is NOT caused by the sun's ultraviolet rays?**

a. Sunburns

b. Skin cancer

c. Holes in the ozone layer

d. Damage to plants and animals

Write the answers in complete sentences.

5 **Why is the ozone layer important?**

_____

6 **What have scientists recently discovered about the ozone layer?**

_____

SHOW YOUR COMPREHENSION

Fill in the chart with the phrases from the box.

The Ozone Layer

What It Is	• It is a thin layer with ❶_____. • It is mostly found between 20 and 30 kilometers above the Earth's surface.
Why It Is Important	• It protects the Earth from ❷_____.
What Scientists Have Discovered	• Some parts of ❸_____. • It appears that ❹_____.

the ozone layer have holes   the sun's harmful ultraviolet rays

the ozone layer can repair itself   a high concentration of ozone gas

SUMMARIZE YOUR READING

Complete the summary with the words from the box.

holes atmosphere ultraviolet rays oxygen atoms

important in size repair consists of

The ozone layer is a part of the Earth's ❶_____. It exists between 20 and 30 kilometers above the Earth's surface. The ozone layer ❷_____ a great deal of ozone, which is made up of three ❸_____. The ozone layer is very ❹_____ because it protects living things on the Earth from the sun's harmful ❺_____. Recently, scientists have found that there are ❻_____ in some parts of the ozone layer. However, the holes seem to increase and decrease ❼_____. This shows that the ozone layer can ❽_____ itself.

THINK & WRITE 3

 How Can We Help Save the Earth?

STEP 1 DISCUSSION **Talk to your partner and answer the questions.**

1. What are some major environmental problems we have?

2. What are some human activities that affect the environment?

STEP 2 ORGANIZATION **Fill in the chart with the phrases from the box.**

try to eat less meat	while brushing our teeth
conserve water	avoid using disposable products
cutting our meat consumption	harmful to the environment

Introduction	There are some simple things we can do to help save the Earth.
Body	**Supporting sentence 1:** We can _____. **Details:** For example, we can take short showers and turn off the tap _____. **Supporting sentence 2:** We can _____. **Details:** They cause a significant amount of waste that is _____. Instead, we can use reusable shopping bags or cups. **Supporting sentence 3:** We can _____. **Details:** It takes a lot of land and energy to produce meat. _____ can help save the Earth.
Conclusion	To help save the Earth, we can conserve water, use fewer disposable products, and eat less meat.

FIRST DRAFT **Complete the writing with the phrases from the chart.**

Title How Can We Help Save the Earth?

There are some simple things we can do to help save the Earth.

First of all, we can _____. For example, we can

take short showers and turn off the tap _____.

Second, we can _____. They cause a significant

amount of waste that is _____. Instead, we can use

reusable shopping bags or cups.

Lastly, we can _____. It takes a lot of land and

energy to produce meat. _____ can help save the

Earth.

To help save the Earth, we can conserve water, use fewer disposable products,

and eat less meat.

STEP 4 **FINAL DRAFT** **Complete the writing. Replace one of the details with you own idea.**

Title _____

There are some simple things we can do to help save the Earth.

First of all, _____

_____

Second, _____

_____

Lastly, _____

_____

To help save the Earth, we can _____

_____

CHAPTER
04

UNIT 13 The Secrets of Stars _ Earth Science

UNIT 14 The Other Stonehenges _ History

UNIT 15 Music in Famous Paintings _ Art & Music

UNIT 16 Helper or Bystander? _ Social Studies

THINK & WRITE 4
Why Do Many Students Not Volunteer?

Subject Earth Science
Topic Stars

The Secrets of Stars

WARM UP

1. How far away from Earth are stars?
2. What colors are the stars in the sky?

BEFORE YOU READ

A   Match the words with the definitions below.

1. _____ extremely   a. to decide
2. _____ distance   b. to a very high degree
3. _____ notice   c. to become aware of
4. _____ temperature   d. a measure of how hot or cold something is
5. _____ determine   e. the amount of space between two places or things

B   Background Knowledge

A star is a hot ball of burning gas made mostly of hydrogen and helium. There are many kinds of stars. They vary in size, age, the amount of heat they produce, and color. The sun is also a star. It is a yellow, medium-sized star. The sun looks so big because it is the closest star to Earth.

Look up at the sky on a clear night. You will likely see a large number of stars. Do you ever wonder about the light from these stars?

There are many interesting facts about the light from stars. First
5 of all, when you see a star, you are actually looking at the past. Stars are **extremely** far away from Earth, so their light takes many years to reach Earth. For example, Proxima Centauri is the closest star to Earth after the sun. Its **distance** from Earth is 4.2 *light years. So if you look at Proxima Centauri tonight, you are seeing what it
10 looked like 4.2 years ago. This is the same for every star in the night sky. You see how it looked years ago.

Look carefully at the stars in the sky. They all seem to be the same. However, if you look a little more closely, you will **notice** that the stars are different colors. Some stars are yellow or white.
15 Other stars are even red or blue. There are several reasons why stars are different colors. The most important reason has to do with their **temperatures**. Cooler stars appear red while stars with higher temperatures are white or blue. The colors of the stars from hottest to coldest are blue, white, yellow, orange, and red. These colors
20 allow astronomers to **determine** the stars' temperatures.   Words 228

***light year** the distance light travels in one year, about 9,460,000,000,000 kilometers

What is the paragraph mainly about?

P2 Why people look at the (future / past) when they look at stars

P3 Why stars are different _____

CHECK YOUR COMPREHENSION

Choose the best answers.

1 What is the passage mainly about?

    a. The life cycles of stars

    b. The history of observing stars

    c. Some facts about light from stars

    d. How to measure distances to stars

2 According to the passage, Proxima Centauri is _____ .

    a. the brightest star

    d. the most beautiful star

    c. the second-closest star to Earth

    d. the smallest star in our solar system

3 According to the passage, what does the color of a star tell us?

    a. Its age

    b. Its size

    c. Its distance from Earth

    d. Its temperature

4 What can be inferred from the passage?

    a. Red stars are hotter than yellow stars.

    b. A star that is blue is very far from Earth.

    c. The colors of stars are invisible without a telescope.

    d. The farther away a star is, the farther in the past we can look.

Write the answers in complete sentences.

5 When you see stars, why are you actually looking at the past?

_____

6 What colors are stars?

_____

SHOW YOUR COMPREHENSION

Fill in the chart with the phrases from the box.

Stars

Distances	• When we see stars, we are ❶_____. • Stars are ❷_____, so light takes a long time to reach Earth. (e.g. Proxima Centauri)
Colors	• Stars are ❸_____. • The colors of stars ❹_____. • From hot to cool, the colors of stars can be blue, white, yellow, orange, and red.

different colors   extremely far away from Earth

actually looking at the past   have to do with their temperatures

SUMMARIZE YOUR READING

Complete the summary with the words from the box.

travel   temperature   yellow   colors

far away   existed   blue   red

There are some interesting facts about the light from stars. When we see a star right now, we are actually looking at the star as it ❶_____ many years ago. The reason is that stars are very ❷_____ from Earth, so their light takes many years to ❸_____ to Earth. In addition, when we look carefully at stars in the sky, we can see various ❹_____. The reason for this color variation is that each star has a different ❺_____. Cooler stars are ❻_____, and warmer ones are orange, ❼_____, or white. The hottest stars shine with ❽_____ light.

Subject History
Topic Prehistoric Megaliths

The Other Stonehenges

WARM UP

1. What do you know about Stonehenge?
2. What ancient monuments are in your country?

▲ Drombeg Stone Circle

BEFORE YOU READ

A **Match the words with the definitions below.**

1. _____ monument   a. in a line
2. _____ megalith   b. complete and not damaged
3. _____ intact   c. a person who studies ancient cultures and people
4. _____ in a row   d. a very large stone, often one used in ancient times
5. _____ archaeologist   e. an old building or place that is important in history

B **Background Knowledge**

Stonehenge is a huge circle of standing stones in Salisbury Plain in Wiltshire, England.
People began building it more than 5,000 years ago. Some of the stones weigh several
tons. And some stones are on top of others. How and why Stonehenge was built are
mysteries today.

Every year, around 800,000 people visit Wiltshire, England. They are visiting Stonehenge. This ancient **monument** of standing stones is at least 5,000 years old. It is the most famous of all the Earth's prehistoric **megaliths**. Yet there are many others around the world.

5　Drombeg Stone Circle is located in southern Ireland. This megalith was created around 1100 B.C. It consists of seventeen stones, and thirteen of them are still **intact**. The stones are about two meters high and are arranged in a circle. Each year during the *winter solstice, the circle lines up perfectly with the sunset.

10　In approximately 4500 B.C., Stone Age people in Brittany, France, began setting up granite stones. There are more than 3,000 stones, called the Carnac Stones, arranged **in rows**. One legend about them claims they were once soldiers but were frozen where they stood. Some historians believe people in the past used a few stones as

15 tombs.

Stone circles do not only exist in Europe. In North America, there are also stone circles. One of the most unusual was discovered in the United States in 2007. This circle of standing stones is located twelve meters below the surface of Lake Michigan. **Archaeologists**

20 discovered a picture of a *mastodon carved on one stone. Some believe the stone circle is more than 10,000 years old.

Most people know more about Stonehenge than other prehistoric megaliths. However, there are mysterious stone circles in many places, including deep in the water. Words 243

* **winter solstice** the shortest day of the year, around December 22
* **mastodon** an animal like an elephant that lived in the past

Q

What is the paragraph mainly about?

P1 What _____ is

P2 How Drombeg Stone Circle (looks / was made)

P3 The Carnac Stones and a(n) _____ about them

P4 A stone circle in (Europe / Lake Michigan)

▲ The Carnac Stones

CHECK YOUR COMPREHENSION

Choose the best answers.

Main Idea   1   **What is the passage mainly about?**

   a. Stonehenge and how it was made

   b. The best prehistoric sites in Europe

   c. The reason people made stone circles

   d. Some ancient megaliths around the world

Details   2   **According to the passage, which megalithic site has more than 3,000 stones?**

   a. Stonehenge

   b. Drombeg Stone Circle

   c. The Carnac Stones

   d. The stone circle in Lake Michigan

3   **There is a picture of a _____ on one of the stones in Lake Michigan.**

   a. tomb

   b. sunset

   c. soldier

   d. mastodon

4   **What can be inferred from the passage?**

   a. Some people still build stone circles today.

   b. Megalithic monuments were important to ancient people.

   c. The same people made Stonehenge and Drombeg Stone Circle.

   d. It was easy for people to build stone circles.

Write the answers in complete sentences.

5   **What is one legend about the Carnac Stones?**

   _____

6   **Where is an unusual stone circle in North America?**

   _____

SHOW YOUR COMPREHENSION

Fill in the chart with the phrases from the box.

	Prehistoric Megaliths
Stonehenge	• Around 800,000 people visit the place each year. • It is ❶_____ at least 5,000 years old. • It is the most famous ❷_____.

Other Prehistoric Megaliths	• Drombeg Stone Circle in Ireland is a stone circle
	  ❸_____.
	• The Carnac Stones are more than 3,000 stones
	  ❹_____.
	• A circle of standing stones in the United States is twelve meters below the surface of Lake Michigan.

arranged in rows	with seventeen stones
prehistoric megalith	a monument of standing stones

SUMMARIZE YOUR READING

Complete the summary with the words from the box.

standing stones	mastodon	sunset	Lake Michigan
megalith	arranged	seventeen	others

Stonehenge is a famous prehistoric ❶_____ that was built at least 5,000 years ago. It is a monument of ❷_____. But there are many ❸_____ around the world. Drombeg Stone Circle in Ireland has ❹_____ stones two meters high. The circle lines up with the ❺_____ during the winter solstice. The Carnac Stones in France are 3,000 stones ❻_____ in rows. And a stone circle in the United States is located twelve meters below the surface of ❼_____. One of the stones has a picture of a(n) ❽_____ on it.

UNIT 15 |
Subject Art & Music
Topic Music in Paintings

Music in Famous Paintings

WARM UP

1. What kinds of paintings do you like?
2. What do artists paint pictures of?

BEFORE YOU READ

A **Match the words with the definitions below.**

1. _____ period   a. to show; to describe
2. _____ flourish   b. an object used to produce music
3. _____ depict   c. to develop quickly and to be successful
4. _____ wipe away   d. a length of time; a certain time in history
5. _____ instrument   e. to remove something by using a cloth or a hand

B **Background Knowledge**

Art movements are periods when artists use a certain style of art. There have been many art movements in history. Renaissance art focused on human beauty and nature. Impressionist artists tried to paint their impressions of the natural world. Cubist art involved creating pictures by using many lines and geometric shapes.

Throughout history, there have been many **periods** of art. There were the Renaissance and the Baroque periods many centuries ago. In the 19th and 20th centuries, Realism, Impressionism, and modern art such as Cubism **flourished**. The art in each period looks
5 different. However, many artists who painted in these periods shared one characteristic. They liked to **depict** music in their paintings.

In 1630, Rembrandt, a famous Dutch Baroque artist, painted *Saul and David*. It shows David playing the harp while King Saul listens to him. In the picture, David's music is clearly having an effect on
10 King Saul as the king is **wiping** tears **away** from his eyes.

Another famous painting with a musician is *The Fifer*. Edouard Manet, a French Impressionist, painted it in 1866. It is a simple painting that shows
15 a young boy playing the fife, which is a kind of flute.

▲ *The Fifer*

In the early 1900s, Cubist art was popular for a while. It became popular mostly because of Pablo Picasso. He
20 made the painting *Three Musicians* in 1921. It shows three musicians with their **instruments**. In 1913, Marc Chagall, who was also a Cubist, painted *The Violinist*. It depicts a man playing the violin with a small town in the background.

These are just a few of the many paintings that show musicians
25 with their instruments. It seems clear that music has been a source of inspiration for many artists.   Words 234

Q

What is the paragraph mainly about?

P1 Different periods of art and a shared _____ of many artists

P2 The painting (*The Fifer* / *Saul and David*)

P3 A painting by _____

P4 Some paintings by (Pablo Picasso / Cubists)

CHECK YOUR COMPREHENSION

Choose the best answers.

Main Idea **1** **What is the main idea of the passage?**

a. There were many different periods of art in the past.

b. Renaissance artists liked to depict music in their paintings.

c. Pablo Picasso is considered one of the greatest artists in history.

d. Music has been depicted in paintings in many different art periods.

Details **2** **Who is mentioned as an artist from the Baroque period?**

a. Rembrandt

b. Edouard Manet

c. Pablo Picasso

d. Marc Chagall

3 **Which of the following is a work by Edouard Manet?**

a. *Saul and David]*

b. *The Fifer*

c. *Three Musicians*

d. *The Violinist*

4 **What do the paintings mentioned in the passage have in common?**

a. They were painted by French artists.

b. They have musicians in them.

c. They are all from the same period of art.

d. They were painted by unknown painters.

Write the answers in complete sentences.

5 **What style of art was popular in the early 1900s?**

_____

6 **What does *The Violinist* show?**

_____

SHOW YOUR COMPREHENSION

Fill in the chart with the phrases from the box.

Music in Famous Paintings

A Shared Characteristic of Many Artists	• Many artists have ❶_____. • It seems that music has been ❷_____ for many artists.
Examples	• ❸_____ shows David playing the harp and King Saul listening to him. • *The Fifer* by Edouard Manet shows a young boy playing the fife. • *Three Musicians* by Pablo Picasso shows three musicians ❹_____. • *The Violinist* by Marc Chagall shows a man playing the violin with a small town in the background.

with their instruments	depicted music in their paintings
a source of inspiration	*Saul and David* by Rembrandt

SUMMARIZE YOUR READING

Complete the summary with the words from the box.

art periods	characteristic	Rembrandt	instruments
different	inspiration	music	Cubist Period

There have been many ❶_____ throughout history. Some of these periods were popular many centuries ago. Others, like the ❷_____, were popular more recently. Although the art of each period looks ❸_____, many artists shared one ❹_____. They liked to depict ❺_____ in their paintings. Artists such as ❻_____, Edouard Manet, Picasso, and Marc Chagall did this by painting musicians with their ❼_____. For example, Chagall's *The Violinist* depicts a man playing the violin. It seems clear that music has been a source of ❽_____ for many artists.

Subject Social Studies
Topic Good Samaritan Laws

Helper or Bystander?

1. Have you ever seen an accident? What happened?
2. What did you do? Did you help anyone?

BEFORE YOU READ

A   Match the words with the definitions below.

1. _____ ignore   a. to steal
2. _____ individual   b. the act of giving help
3. _____ assistance   c. a single person or thing
4. _____ sue   d. to take legal action against someone
5. _____ rob   e. to give no attention to something

B   Background Knowledge

In the Bible, a passerby helped a man whom bandits had attacked. The passerby was called the Good Samaritan. Today, some countries have Good Samaritan laws. These laws protect bystanders. If a bystander helps a person in an accident, the bystander cannot be sued. These laws encourage people to help others.

Imagine that you are driving down a road late at night. You look to the side of the road and see that a car has crashed. There are people in the car, and they seem to be hurt. What will you do in that situation? Will you **ignore** the people and keep driving? Or will you

5 stop your car and try to help the people?

In the past, most people would have instantly stopped to help the injured **individuals**. But people's behavior has changed nowadays. Lots of people are unwilling to offer **assistance**. The reason is that some rescuers injured the people they were trying to save

10 even worse. So the injured people **sued** their would-be rescuers. In some cases, the rescuers had to pay large amounts of money just for trying to help people. Most people do not want to get sued for being nice. These people therefore ignore others in need of assistance.

15 Because so many people are afraid of lawsuits, some countries have passed Good Samaritan laws. The story of the Good Samaritan comes from the Bible. It refers to a person who helped a stranger that had been **robbed** and beaten. Good Samaritan laws provide protection for people who try to help others. Thanks to these laws,

20 people are not allowed to sue anyone who tries to help them. In countries with Good Samaritan laws, people are no longer afraid to help out others.   Words 238

Q

What is the paragraph mainly about?

P1 A situation involving a (car accident / robbery)

P2 Why people are (willing / unwilling) to help others

P3 What the _____ laws are

CHECK YOUR COMPREHENSION

Choose the best answers.

Main Idea **1 What is the passage mainly about?**

    a. Why people should help others

    b. Countries that have Good Samarian laws

    c. Why Good Samaritan Laws have been made

    d. The story in the Bible about the Good Samaritan

Details **2 According to the passage, why are lots of people unwilling to offer assistance?**

    a. They are too busy to help others.

    b. They are worried that they will get hurt.

    c. They are not interested in helping others.

    d. They do not want to get sued for being nice.

3 Good Samaritan laws provide protection for _____.

    a. people who are injured

    b. people who try to help others

    c. people who have been robbed

    d. people whose cars have crashed

4 According to the passage, which is NOT true?

    a. In the past, people were afraid to help others.

    b. People sometimes sue others who try to help them.

    c. Some countries have already passed Good Samaritan laws.

    d. The story of the Good Samaritan comes from the Bible.

Write the answers in complete sentences.

5 What does the Good Samaritan refer to?

_____

6 According to Good Samaritan laws, what are people not allowed to do?

_____

SHOW YOUR COMPREHENSION

Fill in the chart with the phrases from the box.

Good Samaritan Laws

Background	• People were sometimes sued after trying to help others, so they ❶_____.
Purpose	• Good Samaritan laws have been passed in some countries to protect ❷_____.
Effects	• People ❸_____ anyone who tries to help them. • People are no longer ❹_____.

afraid to help out others

are not allowed to sue

people who try to help others

stopped offering assistance

SUMMARIZE YOUR READING

Complete the summary with the words from the box.

Good Samaritan   willing   in need   helped

Bible   ignore   unwilling   sued

In the past, people usually ❶_____ each other when they were injured or ❷_____. These days, people are afraid to help others at times. The reason is that there are cases where an individual was ❸_____ after trying to assist a person in an accident. Most people are afraid of lawsuits and are ❹_____ to help, so they ❺_____ others in need. In some countries, ❻_____ laws have been passed to protect people who try to help others. The name of these laws came from a story in the ❼_____. In countries with these laws, people are more ❽_____ to help others.

THINK & WRITE 4

 Why Do Many Students Not Volunteer?

STEP 1 DISCUSSION **Talk to your partner and answer the questions.**

1. Have you ever helped your community before? What did you do?

2. What kind of volunteer work would you like to do?

STEP 2 ORGANIZATION **Fill in the chart with the phrases from the box.**

have enough information	chatting with their friends
homework and team projects	where and how to volunteer
too busy doing their schoolwork	volunteering is not interesting

Introduction	Many students do not spend enough time volunteering.
Body	**Supporting sentence 1:** They are _____. **Details:** Every day, they have a lot of work to do, such as _____. **Supporting sentence 2:** They do not _____. **Details:** There are many types of volunteer work that they can do. But most students do not know _____. **Supporting sentence 3:** They think _____. **Details:** Students are more interested in fun activities like _____ and watching movies.
Conclusion	Many students do not volunteer because of their busy lives, insufficient information, and the feeling that it is boring.

STEP 3 FIRST DRAFT Complete the writing with the phrases from the chart.

Title   Why Do Many Students Not Volunteer?

Students do not spend enough time volunteering.

First, they are _____. Every day, they have a lot of

work to do, such as _____.

Second, they do not _____. There are many

types of volunteer work that they can do. But most students do not know

_____.

Lastly, they think _____. Students are more

interested in fun activities like _____ and watching

movies.

Many students do not volunteer because of their busy lives, insufficient

information, and the feeling that it is boring.

STEP 4 FINAL DRAFT Complete the writing. Replace one of the details with you own idea.

Title   _____

Students do not spend enough time volunteering.

First, _____

_____

Second, _____

_____

Lastly, _____

_____

Many students do not volunteer because of _____

_____

CHAPTER
05

UNIT 17 **Basic Geometry** _ Math

UNIT 18 **The Imjin War** _ Korean History

UNIT 19 **Forests by the Shore** _ Life Science

UNIT 20 **Is Early Childhood Education Effective?** _ Social Studies

THINK & WRITE 5
How Can We Improve Our English?

UNIT 17

Subject Math
Topic Lines

Basic Geometry

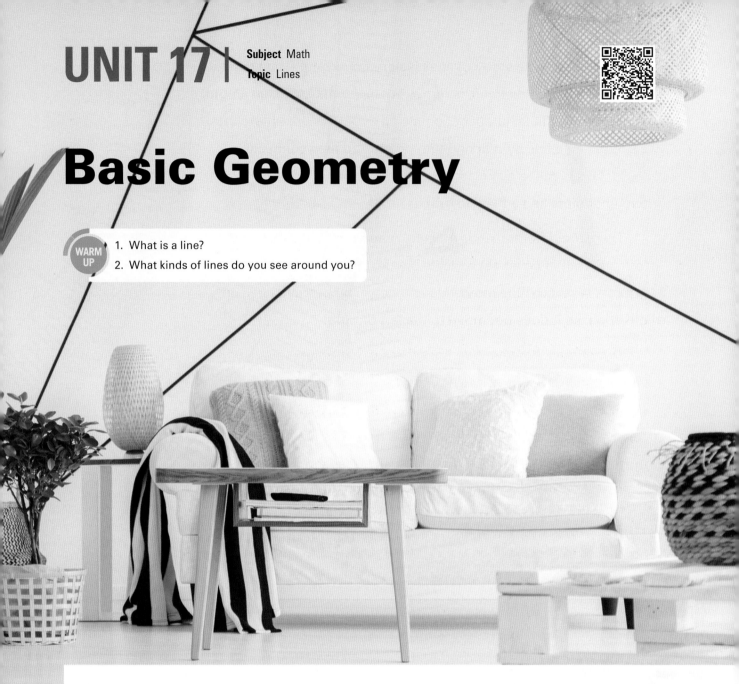

WARM UP

1. What is a line?
2. What kinds of lines do you see around you?

BEFORE YOU READ

A Match the words with the definitions below.

1. _____ infinitely   a. having no limit; endlessly

2. _____ horizontal   b. to cross; to meet at a certain point

3. _____ parallel   c. flat and level with the ground

4. _____ intersect   d. meeting a line or surface at a right angle

5. _____ perpendicular   e. extending in the same direction and not meeting

B Background Knowledge

Geometry is a branch of mathematics. It focuses on the study of the shapes, sizes, and positions of things. Common shapes people study in geometry are squares, circles, and triangles. People often use geometry to find the areas of shapes. They can also measure the volumes of solid shapes.

In geometry, the study of lines is very important. A line extends **infinitely** in two directions, so it has no endpoints and fixed length. There are an infinite number of points on a line. It is possible to make a section on a line by marking two points and then connecting
5 them. This is called a line segment. Unlike a line, a line segment has two endpoints and a fixed length.

There are different kinds of lines. A **horizontal** line moves to the left and right. It never changes its height, so it does not meet the ground. A vertical line moves up and down. It never changes its
10 direction, so it does not move to the left or right.

Sometimes there are two lines that go in the same direction. The distance between these two lines never changes, so these lines never touch each other. These are known as **parallel** lines. On the other hand, two lines may meet. When two lines meet each other,
15 they are called **intersecting** lines. If the intersection of two lines creates a right angle, then these are **perpendicular** lines.

Some lines move in one direction and then change by moving in another direction. Lines that repeatedly change directions are called zigzag lines. Not all lines are straight. For example, a curved line looks like a part of a circle. Words 226

Q

What is the paragraph mainly about?

P1 A line and a(n)
_____

P2 A horizontal and
_____ line

P3 Parallel, (crossing / intersecting), and perpendicular lines.

P4 A zigzag and a (curved / straight) line

▲ Parallel and perpendicular lines

CHECK YOUR COMPREHENSION

Choose the best answers.

Main Idea

1 **What is the passage mainly about?**

a. Different types of lines

b. Why geometry is important

c. How to be good at geometry

d. The difficulty of learning mathematics

Details

2 **How can we make a line segment?**

a. By making lines wide and long

b. By making two lines intersect each other

c. By marking two points and connecting them

d. By extending lines infinitely in two directions

3 **Which types of lines are NOT mentioned in the passage?**

a. Wavy lines

b. Zigzag lines

c. Parallel lines

d. Horizontal lines

4 **According to the passage, which is NOT true of lines?**

a. Parallel lines never meet each other.

b. When two lines meet, they are called infinite lines.

c. When two lines create a right angle, they are perpendicular lines.

d. Zigzag lines are lines that repeatedly change directions.

Write the answers in complete sentences.

5 **What is the difference between a horizontal line and a vertical line?**

_____

6 **What line looks like a part of a circle?**

_____

SHOW YOUR COMPREHENSION

Fill in the chart with the phrases from the box.

Lines in Geometry	
Line vs. **Line Segment**	• A line does not have ❶_____. • A line segment has two endpoints and a fixed length.
Other Types of Lines	• A horizontal line moves ❷_____. • A vertical line moves only up and down. • Parallel lines are lines that go in the same direction and ❸_____. • Intersecting lines are lines that meet each other. • Perpendicular lines are lines ❹_____. • There are also zigzag lines and curved lines.

only to the left and right   endpoints and a fixed length

never touch each other   that intersect at a right angle

SUMMARIZE YOUR READING

Complete the summary with the words from the box.

intersecting   zigzag   fixed length   vertical

horizontal   right angle   touch   end

There are different types of lines in geometry. A line extends in both directions without ❶_____. A line segment is a part of line with two endpoints and a(n) ❷_____. A(n) ❸_____ line goes from left to right while a(n) ❹_____ line moves up and down. Parallel lines are lines that go in the same direction and never ❺_____ each other. If two lines meet at a point, they are called ❻_____ lines. Perpendicular lines are lines that intersect at a(n) ❼_____. Lines that repeatedly change directions are ❽_____ lines, and curved lines look like a part of a circle.

The Imjin War

WARM UP
1. Why do countries fight wars?
2. What are some wars that you know?

▲ Admiral Yi Sun-sin

BEFORE YOU READ

A **Match the words with the definitions below.**

1. _____ enemy
2. _____ invade
3. _____ capture
4. _____ defeat
5. _____ abandon

a. to give up
b. to win against
c. to take control of a place
d. to enter a land to fight the people in it
e. a country that is fighting another country in a war

B **Background Knowledge**

The Imjin War was fought by Korea and Japan. It lasted from 1592 to 1598. The Japanese invaded Korea and attempted to take it over. During the war, Admiral Yi Sun-sin introduced his turtle ships. These powerful ships let the Koreans win naval victories against the Japanese.

Korea and Japan are historically **enemies**. They have fought several wars against each other in the past few centuries. One of these wars happened at the end of the 1500s. From 1592 to 1598, Korea and Japan fought the Imjin War. This war took place on land
5 and at sea.

In the spring of 1592, the Japanese **invaded** the Korean mainland. At this time, Korea was ruled by the Joseon Dynasty. The leader of Korea was King Seonjo. During the early days of the war, the Japanese **captured** Hanyang, which was the capital of
10 the Joseon Dynasty. As a result, the king asked the Chinese Ming Dynasty for assistance.

While the Japanese were initially successful on land, they were less successful at sea. Korean *Admiral Yi Sun-sin **defeated** the Japanese fleet many times. His victories helped prevent the
15 Japanese from providing food and weapons for their forces on the Korean peninsula. Thanks to these victories, Korean land forces, along with soldiers from the Ming Dynasty, were able to defeat the Japanese in several battles and made them leave the peninsula.

From 1593 to 1597, there was a *ceasefire. However, in 1597,
20 the Japanese again invaded Korea. This time, the most important battles took place at sea. Despite having much fewer ships, Admiral Yi's fleet destroyed hundreds of Japanese ships in several battles. This caused the Japanese to depart Korea and to **abandon** their hopes of defeating the country.   Words 238

* **admiral** an officer of very high rank in the navy
* **ceasefire** an agreement to stop fighting for a certain time

Q

What is the paragraph mainly about?

P1 One of the wars fought between Korea and _____

P2 What happened at the (start / end) of the war

P3 How Admiral _____ helped defeat the Japanese

P4 (Where / How) the war came to an end

◀ Yi Sun-sin's turtle ship, *Geobukseon*

CHECK YOUR COMPREHENSION

Choose the best answers.

Main Idea **1** **What is the passage mainly about?**

a. The life of Admiral Yi Sun-sin

b. The wars that happened in Korea

c. Some naval battles during the Joseon Dynasty

d. The war between Korea and Japan from 1592 to 1598

Details **2** **According to the passage, which is NOT true about the Imjin War?**

a. It took place both on land and at sea.

b. It started when Japan invaded Korea.

c. The Japanese eventually won the war.

d. At least three countries were involved in the war.

3 **What happened in 1597?**

a. The Japanese captured Hanyang.

b. Korea and Japan agreed to stop fighting.

c. The Japanese invaded Korea for a second time.

d. The Imjin War ended.

4 **Which is NOT a thing that Admiral Yi Sun-sin did?**

a. He defeated the Japanese fleet.

b. He defeated a Japanese army on the Korean mainland.

c. He prevented the Japanese from supplying their forces in Korea.

d. He caused the Japanese to abandon their hopes of defeating Korea.

Write the answers in complete sentences.

5 **After Hanyang was captured, what did the king do?**

_____

6 **What caused the Japanese to depart Korea completely?**

_____

SHOW YOUR COMPREHENSION

Fill in the chart with the phrases from the box.

The Imjin War

1592	• In the spring, the Japanese invaded the Korean mainland. • The Japanese ❶_____, the capital of the Joseon Dynasty. • The king asked the Ming Dynasty for assistance. • Admiral Yi Sun-sin ❷_____ in naval battles.
1593-1597	• During this time, there was a ceasefire.
1597-1598	• The Japanese ❸_____. • Admiral Yi Sun-sin's fleet destroyed many Japanese ships. • The Japanese abandoned ❹_____.

invaded Korea again   defeated the Japanese

captured Hanyang   their hope of defeating Korea

SUMMARIZE YOUR READING

Complete the summary with the words from the box.

battles fewer ships Joseon Dynasty weapons

leave   ceasefire   defeating   capital

The Imjin War between Korea and Japan happened during the ❶_____.

In 1592, Japan invaded Korea and captured the ❷_____, Hanyang. Korea got

Japan to ❸_____ the peninsula with the help of the Ming Dynasty. In addition,

Admiral Yi Sun-sin prevented the Japanese from supplying their soldiers with food and

❹_____. From 1593 to 1597, there was a ❺_____, but in 1597, the

Japanese invaded Korea again. Despite having ❻_____, Admiral Yi's fleet

destroyed hundreds of Japanese ships in several ❼_____. Finally, in 1598, the

Japanese abandoned their hopes of ❽_____ Korea.

UNIT 19 |

Subject Life Science
Topic Mangrove Forests

Forests by the Shore

WARM UP

1. Where do most trees grow?
2. Why are trees important?

BEFORE YOU READ

A **Match the words with the definitions below.**

1. _____ subtropical   a. to save; to protect

2. _____ tolerate   b. to be able to survive in

3. _____ take in   c. twisted together in an untidy way

4. _____ tangled   d. to absorb something into the body

5. _____ preserve   e. relating to a place that is near a tropical area

B **Background Knowledge**

Mangrove forests are among the world's most diverse ecosystems. More than 1,300 species of animals, including birds, fish, reptiles, amphibians, and mammals, live in them. Every year on July 26, UNESCO celebrates International Day for the Conservation of the Mangrove Ecosystem. It aims to raise awareness of the importance of mangroves and to promote solutions for their conservation.

In some tropical and **subtropical** areas, forests grow on the shore. These are mangrove forests. Mangroves are very unusual trees.

Mangroves can **tolerate** salt water, so they can grow on the
5 shores of oceans and seas. Most of the tree, including the trunk, the branches, and the leaves, grows above the water. The roots are partially above water. But they also go into the water and down into the soil. The roots exposed to air **take in** oxygen. Thick mangrove forests grow on the shores in places in Africa, Asia, Australia, and
10 both Americas.

Mangroves provide many benefits to the environment. First, they prevent shoreline erosion. They protect inland areas from storm surges during typhoons and hurricanes. Beneath the water, their **tangled** roots create unique ecosystems. Many species of
15 fish and marine creatures live in these underwater forests. Above ground, there are many animals, such as birds, monkeys, bats, and even tigers. Mangroves also provide wood, food, and medicine for the people who live near them.

Sadly, mangrove forests are in trouble. In some places,
20 people are starting to develop the land. So they are cutting down mangrove forests. In other places, rising sea levels are making some mangroves die. People are making efforts in many countries to **preserve** their mangrove forests though. The results in some places are promising.

25 Mangrove forests are impressive ecosystems. They provide many advantages. So people must protect these trees.   Words 235

Q

What is the paragraph mainly about?

P1 (How / Where) mangrove forests grow

P2 Why mangrove trees are (unusual / common)

P3 Some _____ of mangrove forests

P4 Some (problems / disadvantages) mangrove forests have

P5 Why people must _____ mangrove forests

CHECK YOUR COMPREHENSION

Choose the best answers.

Main Idea   1   **What is the passage mainly about?**

    a. Trees in tropical and subtropical areas

    b. The largest mangrove forests in the world

    c. Why mangrove trees are important to people

    d. How mangrove forests create unique ecosystems

Details   2   **According to the passage, which is NOT true about mangrove trees?**

    a. They can grow in salt water.

    b. They grow only in a few countries.

    c. They protect the shores from erosion.

    d. They provide places for animals to live.

3   **Some mangrove trees are dying because of** _____.

    a. harmful insects

    b. rising sea levels

    c. dangerous diseases

    d. decreasing temperatures

4   **What can be inferred from the passage?**

    a. Mangrove trees can tolerate cold weather.

    b. Mangrove trees are best for building houses.

    c. Mangrove trees can live for thousands of years.

    d. Mangrove trees are being saved in some countries.

Write the answers in complete sentences.

5   **Why are mangrove roots partially above water?**

_____

6   **How do mangroves help people?**

_____

SHOW YOUR COMPREHENSION

Fill in the chart with the phrases from the box.

Mangrove Forests

Mangrove Trees	• ❶_____ and grow on the shores of oceans and seas • have roots that are partially above water and take in oxygen
Benefits	• protect coastal areas from ❷_____ • ❸_____ for fish and other animals • provide wood, food, and medicine for people
Problems	• are being cut down by ❹_____ • are dying due to rising sea levels

can tolerate salt water   people developing the land

provide a place to live   erosion and storm surges

SUMMARIZE YOUR READING

Complete the summary with the words from the box.

subtropical   rising sea levels   underwater   shores

erosion   preserve   roots   in trouble

Mangrove forests grow in tropical and ❶_____ areas. Mangrove trees can tolerate salt water, so they grow on the ❷_____ of oceans and seas. Most of the trees are above the water, but the ❸_____ are patially above the water and also go into the water. Mangrove forests prevent shoreline ❹_____ and help against storm surges. Fish and other animals live in the ❺_____ forests they create and above the ground. Sadly, mangrove forests are ❻_____. Some people are cutting down mangrove forests to develop the land. ❼_____ are also killing other trees. But people are trying to ❽_____ the forests nowadays.

Subject Social Studies
Topic Early Childhood Education

Is Early Childhood Education Effective?

WARM UP

1. When do most children start attending school?
2. What should young children be learning?

BEFORE YOU READ

A Match the words with the definitions below.

1. _____ preschool
2. _____ supporter
3. _____ improve
4. _____ opponent
5. _____ belong

a. to be in the right place
b. a person who agrees with something
c. a person who disagrees with something
d. to make something better than before
e. a school for children between two and five years of age

B Background Knowledge

In most countries, children attend elementary school at the age of six or seven. But many children attend school before then. Children younger than five usually go to a nursery school or preschool. These schools often follow a play-based learning curriculum rather than academic programs. They also teach children basic reading and writing.

In the past, most children started school at the age of six or seven. Recently, though, some parents are sending children as young as three or four to **preschool**. This is called early childhood education. Many people support it, but others are against it.

5   **Supporters** of early childhood education give many reasons why they like it. Firstly, they claim that children learn a lot by attending preschool at an early age. For instance, young children can learn to read, to do math, and to do other skills. These skills help them when they start elementary school. They also get to spend time with
10 other young children at preschool. That helps them **improve** their social skills. According to studies, these children make friends more easily and cause fewer problems at school.

  Opponents of early childhood education have many reasons for being against it. First of all, they say children who are three
15 and four years old do not **belong** in a school environment. Instead, they should be home with their parents. According to them, young children are not ready to sit at desks and to study like they are in elementary school. They believe it is better for young children to enjoy themselves. They can do that by staying home and by
20 playing. Opponents also think that many preschools are unhealthy environments for young children. They get exposed to many illnesses, so young children at preschools frequently get sick.   Words 238

Q

What is the paragraph mainly about?

P1 How (old / tall) some children are when they start going to preschool

P2 Why some people _____ early childhood education

P3 Why some people are _____ early childhood education

CHECK YOUR COMPREHENSION

Choose the best answers.

<u>Main Idea</u>   1   **What is the passage mainly about?**

a. The best age for kids to start preschool

b. Skills that should be taught at an early age

c. The importance of early childhood education

d. The pros and cons of early childhood education

<u>Details</u>   2   **Which is NOT mentioned as an advantage of early childhood education?**

a. Children learn a lot at an early age.

b. Children can improve their social skills.

c. Children can become healthier.

d. It can be good preparation for school.

3   **What do opponents of early childhood education say?**

a. It only works for a few children.

b. The education fees are too expensive.

c. Children may get bored at school if they learn too much.

d. It is better for young children to stay home and to enjoy themselves.

4   **Parents who think _____ is important may not send their children to preschool.**

a. good health

b. making friends

c. being a good student

d. learning the alphabets

Write the answers in complete sentences.

5   **According to studies, how does spending time with other young children affect children at school?**

_____

6   **Why do opponents of early childhood education say young children do not belong in a school environment?**

_____

SHOW YOUR COMPREHENSION

Fill in the chart with the phrases from the box.

Early Childhood Education	
Meaning	• It means sending ❶_____ to preschool.
Why Supporters Like It	• Children learn a lot by attending preschool. • It helps children ❷_____. • Children make friends more easily and cause fewer problems at school.
Why Opponents Are Against It	• Young children do not belong in a school environment. • They should ❸_____ and play. • Many preschools are ❹_____ for young children.

unhealthy environments	children who are three or four
improve their social skills	be home with their parents

SUMMARIZE YOUR READING

Complete the summary with the words from the box.

disadvantages	young	doing math	get sick
social skills	more easily	unhealthy	playing

There are both advantages and ❶_____ to early childhood education.

Supporters claim that it helps young children start elementary school ❷_____.

Young children can develop abilities such as reading and ❸_____ at preschool.

They can also improve their ❹_____ while playing with other young children.

Opponents of early childhood education say that it is better for young children to stay

home and to enjoy ❺_____. They are too ❻_____ to study like they

are in elementary school. Opponents also say that ❼_____ environments at

preschools can frequently cause young children to ❽_____.

THINK & WRITE 5

 How Can We Improve Our English?

STEP 1 DISCUSSION **Talk to your partner and answer the questions.**

1. How many hours a day do you study English?

2. What do you do to improve your English?

STEP 2 ORGANIZATION **Fill in the chart with the phrases from the box.**

while having fun	watch movies and TV shows
improve our English	playing educational games
expand our vocabulary	reading books is a great way

Introduction	There are several fun and easy ways we can improve our English.
Body	Supporting sentence 1: We can _____. Details: They can help us _____, especially our listening skills and pronunciation. Supporting sentence 2: _____ to learn English. Details: When we read, we can learn correct grammar and _____. Supporting sentence 3: _____ can be helpful. Details: These games allow us to practice English _____.
Conclusion	We can improve our English by watching movies and TV shows, reading books, and playing educational games.

STEP 3 `FIRST DRAFT` **Complete the writing with the phrases from the chart.**

Title   How Can We Improve Our English?

There are several fun and easy ways we can improve our English.

First, we can _____. They can help us

_____, especially our listening skills and pronunciation.

Second, _____ to learn English. When we read, we

can learn correct grammar and _____.

Lastly, _____ can be helpful. These games allow

us to practice English _____.

We can improve our English by watching movies and TV shows, reading

books, and playing educational games.

STEP 4 `FINAL DRAFT` **Complete the writing. Replace one of the details with you own idea.**

Title   _____

There are several fun and easy ways we can improve our English.

First, _____

_____

Second, _____

_____

Lastly, _____

_____

We can improve our English by _____

_____

MEMO

MEMO

MEMO

Reading for Subject

SECOND EDITION

Workbook

2

DARAKWON

School Subject-Integrated Reading Series

Reading for Subject

SECOND EDITION

Subject

Workbook

2

┃ VOCABULARY PRACTICE

A **Write the correct words for the definitions.**

suit	qualified	surface	coast	feature

1. to have as a characteristic

2. the land by the sea or ocean

3. the top layer of water or land

4. a set of clothes worn for a specific activity

5. having the practical knowledge or skills to do something

B **Choose the word that has a meaning similar to the underlined word.**

1. The weather has been <u>fairly</u> cold these days.

   a. quite   b. a little   c. already   d. probably

2. The submarine will <u>descend</u> to the bottom of the ocean.

   a. crash   b. explore   c. go down   d. rise

C **Complete the sentences with the words in the box.**

gear	shallow	stuck	run out of	popularity

1. The mountain climbers must carry a lot of _____.

2. You can stand up easily in _____ water.

3. We are about to _____ milk and eggs.

4. The TV series has gained _____ around the world.

5. The car got _____ in the mud and was unable to move.

▌SENTENCE PRACTICE

D   **Translate the sentences into your language, focusing on the meanings of the underlined parts.**

1. They are not heading into water <u>filled</u> with sharks though.

   _____

2. There are often narrow passages difficult <u>for divers to squeeze</u> between as well.

   _____

3. Sea caves are near the coast <u>while</u> coral caves are in coral reefs.

   _____

4. But <u>those who</u> do dive deep into caves have experiences they will never forget.

   _____

E   **Unscramble the words to complete the sentences.**

1. go / they / about / cave diving / to / are

   _____

2. to do / one percent / are / scuba divers / it / of / only about / qualified

   _____

3. formed / lava tubes / by / caves / are / volcanic activity

   _____

4. fish / in / other caves / living / have / them

   _____

VOCABULARY PRACTICE

A   **Write the correct words for the definitions.**

fingerprint	unique	ray	seek	present

1. a thin beam of light _____

2. to try to find; to look for _____

3. being the only one of its kind _____

4. a mark made by the tip of a person's finger _____

5. to show or state in public _____

B   **Choose the word that has a meaning similar to the underlined word.**

1. Language is an important means of communication.

   a. skill   b. tool   c. source   d. product

2. The clock on the wall is not accurate. It is five minutes fast.

   a. wrong   b. special   c. correct   d. modern

C   **Complete the sentences with the words in the box.**

shape	measure	compare	limitations	proof

1. Before you buy something, you had better _____ the prices.

2. Do you have any _____ that the boy stole the money?

3. A triangle is a _____ that has three sides.

4. He used a ruler to _____ his sister's height.

5. This program is useful, but it also has its _____.

❙ SENTENCE PRACTICE

D **Translate the sentences into your language, focusing on the meanings of the underlined parts.**

1. According to a report from a U.K. newspaper, the shape of your ear <u>could be used</u> as a means of identification.

   _____

2. Then, it <u>compares</u> the scans <u>with</u> the shapes of the ears <u>stored</u> in the system.

   _____

3. Some critics also say that there is no proof <u>that</u> the shapes of a person's ears stay the same.

   _____

4. But <u>with</u> more research, the new technology using ear scans <u>might</u> work better for security systems.

   _____

E **Unscramble the words to complete the sentences.**

1. a system / they / that / ears / invented / scans

   So _____

2. to seek / the ear / the curved parts / image rays / uses / of

   First, the system _____

3. whose / they / finds out / are / it / ears

   Lastly, _____

4. be / at airports / used / people's IDs / can / to check

   The system _____

❙ VOCABULARY PRACTICE

A **Write the correct words for the definitions.**

mathematician	side	area	equal	calculate

1. a line that forms a flat shape _____

2. the same in size, quantity, etc. _____

3. a person who is an expert in mathematics _____

4. to use numbers to find out a total number, amount, etc. _____

5. the amount of surface within a certain space _____

B **Choose the word that has a meaning similar to the underlined word.**

1. The students must figure out the <u>sum</u> of the two numbers added together.

    a. area   b. total   c. height   d. difference

2. Tom <u>described</u> the man he saw to the police.

    a. mentioned   b. brought   c. explained   d. caught

C **Complete the sentences with the words in the box.**

squares	length	missing	value	fields

1. He found the _____ pieces of the puzzle.

2. Draw two _____ and a triangle on the paper.

3. The _____ of this fish is 50 centimeters.

4. How can I find the _____ of X in this equation?

5. Many _____ in psychology deal with the mind, the brain, and behavior.

▌SENTENCE PRACTICE

D   **Translate the sentences into your language, focusing on the meanings of the underlined parts.**

1. It <u>was named after</u> Pythagoras, a Greek mathematician.

   _____

2. <u>Suppose</u> you made three squares on each side of the triangle.

   _____

3. Then, the area of the square on the longest side <u>is equal to</u> the sum of the squares on the other two sides.

   _____

4. Interestingly, Pythagoras is not the only person <u>who</u> discovered this theorem.

   _____

E   **Unscramble the words to complete the sentences.**

1. an interesting fact / the theorem / right triangles / shows / about

   _____

2. the theorem / for / a triangle / useful / the length of / is / calculating / the third side of

   _____

3. you / to know / the other / the lengths of / two sides / need

   Of course, _____

4. try / the length of / to / in the triangle / find / side *c*

   _____

┃ VOCABULARY PRACTICE

A   **Write the correct words for the definitions.**

imperial	calligraphic	former	record	issue

1. previous; in the past   _____

2. relating to fancy handwriting   _____

3. information kept about something that has happened   _____

4. to produce something such as a magazine   _____

5. relating to an empire   (a group of countries ruled by one
    leader)   _____

B   **Choose the word that has a meaning similar to the underlined word.**

1. The snow is <u>gradually</u> starting to fall harder.

    a. often   b. finally   c. slowly   d. suddenly

2. Julia is a very <u>talented</u> pianist and often performs in concerts.

    a. busy   b. pretty   c. famous   d. skilled

C   **Complete the sentences with the words in the box.**

found	policy	scholar	official	precious

1. The _____ is doing research on ancient Egypt.

2. Jane's gold necklace is her most _____ possession.

3. The president will announce the new _____ soon.

4. He hopes to _____ a company sometime next year.

5. Taekwondo is a(n) _____ Olympic sport.

⌶ SENTENCE PRACTICE

D **Translate the sentences into your language, focusing on the meanings of the underlined parts.**

1. It <u>was founded</u> in Changdeok Palace <u>by</u> King Jeongjo in 1776.

   _____

2. It was a place <u>where</u> the writings of former kings and important books were kept.

   _____

3. Although it started as a royal library, the king gradually <u>changed</u> it <u>into</u> a place for studying policies.

   _____

4. Among these young scholars was Jeong Yakyong, a great thinker in the Joseon Period.

   _____

E **Unscramble the words to complete the sentences.**

1. King Jeongjo / of / was / the reforms / the center / of

   The Kyujanggak _____

2. a certain period / the scholars / educated / for / were / and tested / of time

   _____

3. from / them / various / collect and study / made / writings and books / the past

   After that, the king _____

4. took / political partners / and made / as / them / on / political reforms / responsible / them / for

   He also _____

I VOCABULARY PRACTICE

A   **Write the correct words for the definitions.**

persuade	audience	starving	detailed	article

1. very hungry   _____

2. containing a lot of information   _____

3. a piece of writing in a newspaper or magazine   _____

4. a group of people gathered to see or hear something   _____

5. to make someone do something by giving good reasons
   for doing it   _____

B   **Choose the word that has a meaning similar to the underlined word.**

1. Facial expressions do not always match a person's true <u>emotions</u>.

   a. words   b. wishes   c. feelings   d. passions

2. His salary is not <u>sufficient</u> to support his family.

   a. low   b. stable   c. useless   d. enough

C   **Complete the sentences with the words in the box.**

interest	impression	bully	cites	convince

1. It is not nice to _____ other people.

2. She tried to _____ her parents that she was not lying.

3. He often _____ important information in his speeches.

4. Tell funny stories to maintain the listeners' _____.

5. Kevin usually makes a good _____ on people.

┃ SENTENCE PRACTICE

D **Translate the sentences into your language, focusing on the meanings of the underlined parts.**

1. First of all, <u>the more</u> you know about your audience, <u>the better</u> your speech will be.

   _____

2. If you want to <u>persuade people to do</u> volunteer work in the community, focus on what types of work they can do.

   _____

3. They will <u>be</u> more <u>likely to</u> remember your speech if you <u>make them experience</u> a strong emotion.

   _____

4. You can show some statistics or cite a newspaper article about how many students <u>are being bullied</u> these days.

   _____

E **Unscramble the words to complete the sentences.**

1. how / can / talk / they / a difference / make / about

   You could also _____

2. telling / a story / your audience / will inspire / try / them / that

   In addition, _____

3. a speech / you / giving / bullying / imagine / are / about

   _____

4. should / you / convince / help / your audience

   They _____

❘ VOCABULARY PRACTICE

A   **Write the correct words for the definitions.**

enormous	expand	landform	steep	affect

1. to become greater in size or amount   _____

2. very large; huge   _____

3. rising or falling at a sharp angle   _____

4. to cause something to change in some way   _____

5. a natural shape on the Earth's surface   _____

B   **Choose the word that has a meaning similar to the underlined word.**

1. There are <u>numerous</u> books in the library.

   a. old   b. a few   c. many   d. interesting

2. The view from the <u>peak</u> of the mountain is amazing.

   a. top   b. side   c. rock   d. bottom

C   **Complete the sentences with the words in the box.**

capable	contract	hemisphere	valley	contain

1. The river runs through the _____.

2. A _____ is exactly one half of the Earth.

3. Some metals _____ when they get hot.

4. Juices and soda _____ a lot of sugar.

5. My sister is _____ of swimming very fast.

▌SENTENCE PRACTICE

D   **Translate the sentences into your language, focusing on the meanings of the underlined parts.**

1.   Glaciers are enormous sheets of ice and snow <u>which</u> form in cold areas.

   _____

2.   They <u>are capable of</u> moving in various directions <u>as</u> they expand and contract.

   _____

3.   Fjords are deep, narrow valleys <u>flooded</u> by seawater.

   _____

4.   The Great Lakes in the United States and Canada are five huge lakes <u>containing</u> around 20 percent of the world's liquid fresh water.

   _____

E   **Unscramble the words to complete the sentences.**

1.   type / one / are / of glacial landform / well-known / fjords

   _____

2.   by / can also / forming / the shapes of / affect / mountains / horns

   Glaciers _____

3.   than / stands / 4,400 meters / more / high

   The Matterhorn in the Alps in Europe _____

4.   formed / glaciers / can / by / as well / be

   Lakes _____

I VOCABULARY PRACTICE

A   **Write the correct words for the definitions.**

artwork	detergent	canvas	represent	look back

1. a soap used for cleaning clothes   _____

2. to be a symbol of something   _____

3. to think about something in the past   _____

4. a work of art, especially one in a museum   _____

5. a type of material on which artists paint pictures   _____

B   **Choose the word that has a meaning similar to the underlined word.**

1. The man is holding a large <u>object</u> in his hands.

    a. box   b. animal   c. thing   d. picture

2. His latest work has been <u>attacked</u> by critics.

    a. stolen   b. praised   c. developed   d. criticized

C   **Complete the sentences with the words in the box.**

actress	bill	exhibition	collector	valuable

1. This large diamond is very _____.

2. Susan is a(n) _____ in the play at the theater.

3. Mr. Johnson is a(n) _____ of modern art.

4. Ali found a hundred-dollar _____ on the street.

5. I have two tickets for the photo _____ by Robert Capa.

▌SENTENCE PRACTICE

D **Translate the sentences into your language, focusing on the meanings of the underlined parts.**

1. He made silkscreen artwork <u>which</u> featured dollar bills, detergent boxes, soup cans, bananas, and other similar objects.

   _____

2. He said <u>it</u> was great <u>that</u> the richest and the poorest bought the same things in America.

   _____

3. For example, a famous actor pays <u>the same</u> amount of money <u>as</u> a poor man does to buy a Coke.

   _____

4. <u>Since</u> Warhol died, many books, films, and exhibitions <u>have looked back at</u> him and his art.

   _____

E **Unscramble the words to complete the sentences.**

1. the / pop artist / was / most / the 1960s / famous / in

   Andy Warhol _____

2. why / made / was / he / pop art

   That _____

3. founded / Warhol / called / the Factory / a studio

   During the 1960s, _____

4. Warhol / consumerism / by / attacked / his art / saying / represented / that

   They _____

I VOCABULARY PRACTICE

A   **Write the correct words for the definitions.**

medical	hormone	gain weight	lose weight	quality

1. to become heavier   _____

2. to become thinner or lighter   _____

3. relating to the treatment of illnesses and injuries   _____

4. how good or bad something is   _____

5. a chemical produced by certain cells in the body   _____

B   **Choose the word that has a meaning similar to the underlined word.**

1. Doctors believe the man's illness is <u>linked</u> to his diet.

   a. moved   b. grown   c. exposed   d. connected

2. Tom tried to <u>suppress</u> his anger but couldn't.

   a. hide   b. forget   c. control   d. express

C   **Complete the sentences with the words in the box.**

appetite	result in	according to	useless	deeply

1. She had loss of _____ and lost a lot of weight.

2. You should stop spending money on _____ things.

3. _____ the teacher, Mark is the best student.

4. He usually sleeps so _____ that he does not hear the alarm.

5. Eating too much may _____ a person becoming overweight.

I SENTENCE PRACTICE

D   **Translate the sentences into your language, focusing on the meanings of the underlined parts.**

1.   Leptin suppresses appetite by <u>making people feel</u> full.

   _____

2.   However, this is only true for people <u>who</u> do not sleep enough.

   _____

3.   For example, <u>getting</u> 7 hours of bad sleep a night is useless.

   _____

4.   If people <u>have difficulty sleeping</u> deeply, getting enough sleep will not <u>help them lose</u> weight.

   _____

   _____

E   **Unscramble the words to complete the sentences.**

1.   a relationship / there / sleep and / between / weight

   Is _____

2.   closely / appetite hormones / linked / are / and

   Sleep _____

3.   they / hungry / control / or full / feel / people / how

   _____

4.   of sleep / needs / 7 hours / the human body / a day / at least

   _____

| VOCABULARY PRACTICE

A **Write the correct words for the definitions.**

| recently | available | virtual | allow | prefer |

1. not long ago _____

2. to give permission for someone do something _____

3. ready or able to be used _____

4. to like one thing more than another _____

5. made on a computer rather than in the real world _____

B **Choose the word that has a meaning similar to the underlined word.**

1. I gave her the letter in person.

    a. gladly   b. secretly   c. personally   d. surprisingly

2. The teacher showed one method to solve the problem.

    a. way   b. answer   c. question   d. style

C **Complete the sentences with the words in the box.**

| collection | explore | view | statue | mummies |

1. I made a(n) _____ of a lion from a piece of wood.

2. Sue has a small _____ of ancient coins.

3. Egypt is famous for _____ and pyramids.

4. You can _____ the whole city from the top of the tower.

5. It is a lot of fun to _____ new places.

I SENTENCE PRACTICE

D   **Translate the sentences into your language, focusing on the meanings of the underlined parts.**

1.   There are other ways <u>to see</u> these works up close though.

    _____

2.   Museums and galleries <u>have been putting</u> their collections online recently.

    _____

3.   VR creates a computer-generated world and <u>lets people explore</u> it.

    _____

4.   Both methods <u>allow people to view</u> art.

    _____

E   **Unscramble the words to complete the sentences.**

1.   interested in / a virtual tour / people / Renaissance art / can / of the Vatican Museums / take

    _____

2.   they / or smartphone / a desktop computer / need / laptop / is

    All _____

3.   it / to travel / is not / anymore / to see / necessary / art

    Thanks to modern technology, _____

4.   tours / almost like / they / go on / that are / can / the real thing

    Then, _____

❙ VOCABULARY PRACTICE

A   **Write the correct words for the definitions.**

expert	indoors	insect	disease	primary

1. inside a building   _____

2. an illness   _____

3. main; most important   _____

4. a person with special knowledge of something   _____

5. a small creature with six legs and a body divided into
    three parts   _____

B   **Choose the word that has a meaning similar to the underlined word.**

1. The shoes are <u>currently</u> on sale for 30 percent off.

    a. now   b. still   c. already   d. especially

2. <u>A number of</u> people showed up at the park to help clean it.

    a. Few   b. Every   c. Many   d. Several

C   **Complete the sentences with the words in the box.**

steadily	urbanization	exposure	recycle	commonplace

1. It is important to _____ glass, metal, and plastic.

2. The weather is _____ getting colder these days.

3. Cows and chickens are _____ on farms.

4. _____ is reducing the amount of farmland in the world.

5. Too much _____ to the sun can cause sunburn.

❙ SENTENCE PRACTICE

D **Translate the sentences into your language, focusing on the meanings of the underlined parts.**

1. Due to industrial development and urbanization, the amount of farmland is decreasing.

   _____

2. To solve this problem, vertical farming was invented.

   _____

3. Greenhouses have just one level while vertical farms have many levels.

   _____

4. People can produce more food in limited amounts of space, which is the primary goal of vertical farming.

   _____

E **Unscramble the words to complete the sentences.**

1. seven billion / the world's population / currently / than / is / people / more

   _____

2. allows / this / grow / all year round / to / crops

   _____

3. less / is / to / and diseases / exposure / insects / there / harmful

   _____

4. able / their own / grow / people in cities / crops / are now / to

   Thanks to vertical farms, _____

| VOCABULARY PRACTICE

A   Write the correct words for the definitions.

| custom | typically | weave | bead | arrowhead |

1. usually; normally   _____

2. the sharp, pointed end of an arrow   _____

3. a small, round object with a hole through it   _____

4. a habit or practice often followed by many people   _____

5. to form by connecting thread or another material   _____

B   Choose the word that has a meaning similar to the underlined word.

1. Some people used magic symbols to <u>keep away</u> evil spirits.

    a. call   b. fight   c. avoid   d. protect

2. The UFO suddenly went faster and then <u>vanished</u> in the night sky.

    a. shone   b. stopped   c. traveled   d. disappeared

C   Complete the sentences with the words in the box.

| tribe | prevented | decorate | feather | place |

1. The rain _____ us from go hiking.

2. The child found a bird's _____ on the ground.

3. The _____ lives deep in the rainforest.

4. _____ the food in the refrigerator after dinner.

5. The children helped _____ the Christmas tree.

❙ SENTENCE PRACTICE

D   **Translate the sentences into your language, focusing on the meanings of the underlined parts.**

1. They welcomed good dreams but wanted to <u>prevent people from having</u> bad dreams.

    _____

2. The hoop was typically a twig from a willow tree <u>that</u> was bent into a circle.

    _____

3. <u>Once</u> the dream catcher was completed, it was placed over a person's bed.

    _____

4. It would <u>let good dreams pass</u> through the holes in the web while the person slept.

    _____

E   **Unscramble the words to complete the sentences.**

1. one / was / the largest / of / Native Americans / groups of

    _____ the Ojibwe tribe.

2. could / the Ojibwe people / it / bad dreams / believed / keep away

    _____

3. were all / a hoop design / based / they / on

    _____

4. woven / so it / in the center / a spider web / was / looked like

    String _____

▌ VOCABULARY PRACTICE

A   **Write the correct words for the definitions.**

| consist of | thin | Arctic | appear | decrease |

1. to seem   _____

2. not thick   _____

3. to be made up of   _____

4. the part of the Earth near the North Pole   _____

5. to become less in number or amount   _____

B   **Choose the word that has a meaning similar to the underlined word.**

1. We should <u>divide</u> the pizza into six pieces.

    a. make   b. eat   c. split   d. cook

2. He <u>repaired</u> his computer by himself.

    a. broke   b. fixed   c. bought   d. sold

C   **Complete the sentences with the words in the box.**

| breathe | atoms | ultraviolet | exists | sunburns |

1. People living in big cities cannot _____ clean air.

2. An electron microscope can see individual _____.

3. Do you believe that life _____ on other planets?

4. The sun's _____ rays can be blocked if you wear a hat.

5. I got _____ because I played on the beach for too long.

▌SENTENCE PRACTICE

D **Translate the sentences into your language, focusing on the meanings of the underlined parts.**

1. The Earth's atmosphere consists of the air <u>that</u> covers the planet from the surface to outer space.

   _____

2. <u>It</u> is these ultraviolet rays <u>that</u> cause people to get sunburns and skin cancer.

   _____

3. <u>Without</u> the ozone layer, ultraviolet rays <u>would hurt</u> or <u>kill</u> most of the plants and animals that live on the planet.

   _____

4. <u>So long as</u> the ozone layer exists, humans—and other forms of life—will be safe.

   _____

E **Unscramble the words to complete the sentences.**

1. can / several / divided / the atmosphere / into / be / different layers

   _____

2. we / two / the oxygen / is / atoms / breathe / that / made up of

   _____

3. itself / appears / can / it / that / repair / the ozone layer

   Fortunately, _____

4. the Earth / of / protects / the harmful / the sun / ultraviolet rays / from

   This layer _____

┃ VOCABULARY PRACTICE

A   **Write the correct words for the definitions.**

likely	wonder	reach	have to do with	astronomer

1. probably _____

2. to arrive at a place _____

3. to want to know about _____

4. a scientist who studies the stars, planets, etc. _____

5. to be related to something _____

B   **Choose the word that has a meaning similar to the underlined word.**

1. It is <u>extremely</u> difficult to get a perfect score on the test.

    a. never   b. always   c. highly   d. exactly

2. We must <u>determine</u> where to have the picnic this weekend.

    a. ask   b. vote   c. discuss   d. decide

C   **Complete the sentences with the words in the box.**

past	far away	distance	noticed	temperature

1. My uncle lives _____ from my house.

2. This morning, the _____ dropped to 10 degrees below zero.

3. We cannot change the _____, but we can learn from it.

4. I _____ Mary was wearing new glasses.

5. Five kilometers is a long _____ to walk.

I SENTENCE PRACTICE

D   **Translate the sentences into your language, focusing on the meanings of the underlined parts.**

1. Stars are extremely far away from Earth, so their light <u>takes many years to reach</u> Earth.

   _____

2. If you look at Proxima Centauri tonight, you are seeing <u>what it looked like</u> 4.2 years ago.

   _____

3. Cooler stars appear red <u>while</u> stars with higher temperatures are white or blue.

   _____

4. These colors <u>allow astronomers to determine</u> the stars' temperatures.

   _____

E   **Unscramble the words to complete the sentences.**

1. the sun / closest / is / to Earth / after / the / star

   Proxima Centauri _____

2. be / to / the same / seem / they all

   _____

3. are / why / several reasons / there / colors / are / stars / different

   _____

4. important / has / with / to / the most / temperatures / do / reason / their

   _____

VOCABULARY PRACTICE

A **Write the correct words for the definitions.**

prehistoric	arrange	legend	unusual	carve

1. not common or ordinary _____

2. a story coming down from the past _____

3. to place things in a particular order or position _____

4. from the time before recorded history _____

5. to cut a pattern or letter on the surface of something _____

B **Choose the word that has a meaning similar to the underlined word.**

1. The vase fell on the ground, but it was <u>intact</u>.

   a. valuable   b. unbroken   c. beautiful   d. damaged

2. The population of the city is <u>approximately</u> 1.5 million people.

   a. exactly   b. up to   c. roughly   d. almost

C **Complete the sentences with the words in the box.**

monument	in rows	tomb	soldiers	mysterious

1. Who is buried in this _____?

2. Many _____ were wounded in the battle.

3. We saw some _____ lights in the sky.

4. Put the boxes _____ on the floor.

5. The Leaning Tower of Pisa is a famous _____ in Italy.

┃ SENTENCE PRACTICE

D Translate the sentences into your language, focusing on the meanings of the underlined parts.

1. There are more than 3,000 stones, <u>called</u> the Carnac Stones, <u>arranged</u> in rows.

2. One legend about them claims they were once soldiers but were frozen <u>where</u> they stood.

3. Archaeologists discovered a picture of a mastodon <u>carved</u> on one stone.

4. However, there are mysterious stone circles in many places, <u>including</u> deep in the water.

E Unscramble the words to complete the sentences.

1. all the Earth's / is / the most / of / prehistoric megaliths / famous

   It _____

2. was / 1100 B.C. / this megalith / around / created

   _____

3. during / lines up / the winter solstice / perfectly with / the circle

   Each year _____ the sunset.

4. people in the past / believe / tombs / as / a few stones / used

   Some historians _____

VOCABULARY PRACTICE

A   **Write the correct words for the definitions.**

| century | characteristic | effect | source | inspiration |

1. a result of an action

2. one hundred years

3. a quality or feature of a person or thing

4. something that gives a person new, creative ideas

5. a place, person, or thing that you get something from

B   **Choose the word that has a meaning similar to the underlined word.**

1. There have been many different <u>periods</u> of history.

   a. times   b. events   c. people   d. wars

2. His painting <u>depicts</u> a couple walking on the beach.

   a. looks   b. faces   c. shows   d. explains

C   **Complete the sentences with the words in the box.**

| throughout | flourished | tears | instrument | musician |

1. Janet is a(n) _____ in an orchestra.

2. He has helped the poor _____ his life.

3. The piano is the most popular _____ in the world.

4. _____ poured down her cheeks as she heard the story.

5. Impressionism _____ in France in the late 19th century.

I SENTENCE PRACTICE

D **Translate the sentences into your language, focusing on the meanings of the underlined parts.**

1. In the picture, David's music is clearly having an effect on King Saul <u>as</u> the king is wiping tears away from his eyes.

_____

2. It is a simple painting that shows a young boy playing the fife<u>, which</u> is a kind of flute.

_____

3. It depicts a man playing the violin <u>with a small town in the background</u>.

_____

4. <u>It</u> seems clear <u>that</u> music has been a source of inspiration for many artists.

_____

E **Unscramble the words to complete the sentences.**

1. there / art / been / periods of / have / history / many

    Throughout _____

2. in these periods / one / many artists / shared / who painted / characteristic

    However, _____

3. listens to / shows / while King Saul / David / playing / him / the harp

    It _____

4. of / popular / mostly / Pablo Picasso / became / because

    It _____

VOCABULARY PRACTICE

A   **Write the correct words for the definitions.**

| bystander | injured | would-be | unwilling | lawsuit |

1. physically hurt   _____

2. not wanting to do something   _____

3. potential; possible   _____

4. a problem brought to a court of law to be solved   _____

5. a person who watches what is happening without taking part in that activity   _____

B   **Choose the word that has a meaning similar to the underlined word.**

1. He pushed a button, and the TV <u>instantly</u> turned off.

    a. finally   b. quietly   c. accidently   d. immediately

2. The doctor provided <u>assistance</u> to the person in the accident.

    a. money   b. advice   c. help   d. operation

C   **Complete the sentences with the words in the box.**

| ignored | behavior | rescuer | sue | robbed |

1. He _____ his father's advice.

2. Please improve your _____ in class.

3. He will _____ the person who spread the rumor.

4. The _____ helped save five people's lives.

5. The police caught the man after he _____ the bank.

I SENTENCE PRACTICE

D **Translate the sentences into your language, focusing on the meanings of the underlined parts.**

1. In the past, most people <u>would have</u> instantly <u>stopped</u> to help the injured individuals.

_____

2. <u>The reason is that</u> some rescuers injured the people they were trying to save even worse.

_____

3. It refers to a person who helped a stranger that <u>had been robbed</u> and <u>beaten</u>.

_____

4. Thanks to these laws, people <u>are not allowed to</u> sue anyone who tries to help them.

_____

E **Unscramble the words to complete the sentences.**

1. people / unwilling / offer / are / assistance / to

   Lots of _____

2. for / most people / get sued / want to / nice / do not / being

   _____

3. others / these people / in need of / ignore / assistance

   _____

4. help out / people / longer / are / no / afraid / others / to

   In countries with Good Samaritan laws, _____

VOCABULARY PRACTICE

A   Write the correct words for the definitions.

| extend | fixed | section | repeatedly | straight |

1. a part of something larger _____

2. to stretch out _____

3. not able to be changed _____

4. without a bend, curve, or angle _____

5. again and again _____

B   Choose the word that has a meaning similar to the underlined word.

1. A line can stretch <u>infinitely</u> in two directions.

   a. quickly   b. carefully   c. correctly   d. endlessly

2. The two roads <u>intersect</u> next to the park.

   a. start   b. end   c. cross   d. curve

C   Complete the sentences with the words in the box.

| direction | mark | height | is known as | circle |

1. It is not easy to draw a perfect _____.

2. The road heads in a northeast _____.

3. Did you _____ Jane's birthday on the calendar?

4. The average _____ of the girls in the class is 157 centimeters.

5. Greg _____ a very friendly person.

❙ SENTENCE PRACTICE

D **Translate the sentences into your language, focusing on the meanings of the underlined parts.**

1. It is possible <u>to make</u> a section on a line by marking two points and then connecting them.

   _____

2. Sometimes there are two lines <u>that</u> go in the same direction.

   _____

3. <u>Not all</u> lines are straight.

   _____

4. For example, a curved line <u>looks like</u> a part of a circle.

   _____

E **Unscramble the words to complete the sentences.**

1. of / a line / are / points / an infinite number / on

   There _____

2. between / changes / the distance / these two lines / never

   _____

3. known / parallel lines / are / these / as

   _____

4. are / zigzag lines / change / called / that repeatedly / directions

   Lines _____

▌VOCABULARY PRACTICE

A   **Write the correct words for the definitions.**

mainland	capital	fleet	weapon	battle

1. a group of ships in a country's navy _____

2. a fight between two military forces _____

3. the city where the government of a country is _____

4. the biggest part of the land in a country _____

5. an object used for fighting or attacking someone _____

B   **Choose the word that has a meaning similar to the underlined word.**

1. <u>Initially</u>, he thought he would stay in the U.S. for a year.

   a. Luckily   b. At first   c. Certainly   d. Suprisingly

2. Our team was able to <u>defeat</u> our rival in baseball.

   a. help   b. hurt   c. change   d. win against

C   **Complete the sentences with the words in the box.**

enemies	invade	peninsula	departs	abandon

1. The flight for Jeju Island _____ at 3:00 p.m.

2. Korea is a(n) _____ surrounded by the sea on three sides.

3. Tom decided to _____ his studies and to find a job.

4. Snakes and frogs are natural _____.

5. The army will _____ the island tomorrow.

┃ SENTENCE PRACTICE

D ┃ **Translate the sentences into your language, focusing on the meanings of the underlined parts.**

1. During the early days of the war, the Japanese captured Hanyang, <u>which</u> was the capital of the Joseon Dynasty.

2. His victories helped <u>prevent the Japanese from providing</u> food and weapons for their forces on the Korean peninsula.

3. <u>Despite</u> having much fewer ships, Admiral Yi's fleet destroyed hundreds of Japanese ships in several battles.

4. This <u>caused the Japanese to depart</u> Korea and <u>to abandon</u> their hopes of defeating the country.

E ┃ **Unscramble the words to complete the sentences.**

1. one of / at the end of / these wars / happened / the 1500s

2. at / this war / and / land / sea / took place on

3. the Joseon Dynasty / ruled / Korea / by / was

   At this time, _____

4. asked / for / the Chinese Ming Dynasty / assistance

   As a result, the king _____

❙ VOCABULARY PRACTICE

A   **Write the correct words for the definitions.**

shore	erosion	storm surge	ecosystem	impressive

1. amazing; awesome   _____

2. the land next to the sea or ocean   _____

3. all the plants and animals in a certain area   _____

4. the rising of the level of the sea during a storm   _____

5. the process by which rock or soil is gradually destroyed   _____
    by wind, rain, etc.

B   **Choose the word that has a meaning similar to the underlined word.**

1. It is important to <u>preserve</u> the world's natural resources.

    a. use   b. protect   c. develop   d. discover

2. The outlook for this business does not look <u>promising</u>.

    a. clear   b. positive   c. complex   d. effective

C   **Complete the sentences with the words in the box.**

tolerate	take in	thick	marine	in trouble

1. _____ animals like seals and sea lions live there.

2. Tropical plants do not generally _____ cold temperatures.

3. The resort is surrounded by high mountains and _____ forests.

4. If you _____ more calories than you use, you will gain weight.

5. George is _____ because he lied to his parents.

▎SENTENCE PRACTICE

D **Translate the sentences into your language, focusing on the meanings of the underlined parts.**

1. The roots <u>exposed</u> to air take in oxygen.

_____

2. They <u>protect</u> inland areas <u>from</u> storm surges during typhoons and hurricanes.

_____

3. Mangroves also <u>provide</u> wood, food, and medicine <u>for</u> the people who live near them.

_____

4. People are making efforts in many countries <u>to preserve</u> their mangrove forests though.

_____

E **Unscramble the words to complete the sentences.**

1. provide / mangroves / many benefits / the environment / to

_____

2. in / mangrove forests / trouble / are

Sadly, _____

3. people / develop / starting / the land / to / are

In some places, _____

4. some mangroves / rising sea levels / making / die / are

In other places, _____

I VOCABULARY PRACTICE

A   **Write the correct words for the definitions.**

childhood	education	support	be against	attend

1.   regularly to go to a place _____

2.   the process of teaching and learning _____

3.   to agree with something _____

4.   to disagree with something _____

5.   the time when a person is a child _____

B   **Choose the word that has a meaning similar to the underlined word.**

1.   Jason always tries to improve his skills and abilities.

a. learn   b. practice   c. develop   d. talk about

2.   The teacher frequently asks her students some questions.

a. sometimes   b. often   c. rarely   d. always

C   **Complete the sentences with the words in the box.**

claim	knowledge	cause	belong	illnesses

1.   The loud children _____ many problems in class.

2.   You can expand your _____ at the library.

3.   Colds and the flu are not usually serious _____.

4.   Some people _____ that aliens are real.

5.   The piano does not _____ in the small room.

I SENTENCE PRACTICE

D   **Translate the sentences into your language, focusing on the meanings of the underlined parts.**

1. Some parents are sending children <u>as young as</u> three or four to preschool.

   _____

2. They claim that children learn a lot <u>by attending</u> preschool at an early age.

   _____

3. Young children are not ready to sit at desks and to study <u>like</u> they are in elementary school.

   _____

4. They believe <u>it</u> is better <u>for young children to enjoy</u> themselves.

   _____

E   **Unscramble the words to complete the sentences.**

1. spend / other young children / get to / preschool / with / time / at

   They also _____

2. them / helps / their social skills / that / improve

   _____

3. for / early childhood education / of / have / against it / many reasons / being

   Opponents _____

4. are / belong / who / three and four years old / a school environment / do not / in

   Children _____

MEMO

MEMO

MEMO

Reading for Subject